VI

'There is no way out ... Once a Catholic, always a Catholic and all that.'
Noreen O'Carroll, *The Irish Times*, 23 April 1997

'I wonder could she expand on the "and all that"?'
Virginia Kennerley, *The Irish Times*, 5 May 1997

Noreen O'Carroll

Virginia's Questions
Why I am still a Catholic

the columba press

First published in 1998 by
the columba press
55a Spruce Avenue, Stillorgan Industrial Park
Blackrock, Co Dublin

Cover by Bill Bolger
The cover picture is a detail from *The Starry Night* by
Vincent Van Gogh. Museum of Modern Art, New York.
Origination by The Columba Press
Printed in Ireland by Colour Books Ltd, Dublin
ISBN 1 85607 218 5

Contents

CHAPTER 1

The Challenge

It all began in a manner which did not concern me at all. In the spring of 1997 while visiting Rome, President Mary Robinson had a private audience with Pope John Paul II in the Vatican. There was, I recall, a brief report of her visit in *The Irish Times*, and probably in some other papers too, and I think also on the evening television news. Shortly afterwards a brief letter appeared in *The Irish Times* written by a Fr David O'Hanlon with an address at the Irish College in Rome. Fr O'Hanlon was sharply critical of President Robinson's dress during her meeting with the Pope and concluded his letter by stating that she was 'cheap'. Within days another brief letter appeared, signed by a group of priests disassociating themselves from both the content and tone of Fr O'Hanlon's letter. These were the subject of much discussion at the Milltown Institute where I teach philosophy. One particularly heated exchange took place among the second-year philosophy students after one of my classes and passionate words were uttered by a seminarian, who supported the stance of Fr O'Hanlon, and a few of the lay women students.

The following Saturday 19 April I went to a patristic seminar in St Patrick's College, Maynooth. Arriving minutes early, I sat in the car and glanced through that day's *Irish Times*. A large photograph of President Robinson and the Pope caught my eye. The headline accompanying both the photograph and an article by Fr David O'Hanlon startled me. 'Attempt to provoke a last bang of the crozier failed to work' it proclaimed. Sensing something strange and disturbing about the piece I read through it. The gist of Fr O'Hanlon's article was an extended version of his earlier letter. His polemic against President Robinson was anchored in his disapproval of the colour and style of the dress she wore when she met the Pope. On that occasion, President Robinson had worn a green outfit with a sprig of mimosa on a brooch, since it was March 8, Women's Day, and mimosa is traditionally given by Italian husbands, boyfriends and sons to their womenfolk to wear on that day. However, Fr O'Hanlon was offended by the President's attire at her private meeting with the Pope because, he maintained, Vatican protocol for both sexes during such visits is simply *abito scuro* (literally, sombre dress – black, grey or navy, and little or no jewellery). And from her choice of outfit, Fr O'Hanlon inferred that President Robinson had deliberately set out to insult the Pope and the Roman Catholic Church stating: 'But I suspect, as is widely rumoured in Irish circles here in Rome, that Mary Robinson, when she had at last to meet the Pope, hoped to manipulate the situation by provoking the Vatican either to turn her away on account of her dress (as happened to Princess – now Queen – Paola of Belgium in 1962), or at least to condemn modern Ireland in her presence for recent socio-legal trends. This, then, in either case, might fruitfully be represented to the Irish people as the ultimate bang of a crozier for all that post-Catholic Ireland has become, and the last gasp of a desperate, discredited, rigid, reactionary and patriarchal regime'. And he concluded his article with the statement: 'And I say it again – cheap, cheap and unworthy, if not of you, at least of our President! I might lastly add, for the benefit of those who cleverly see but foolishly let slip the non-ordination of women as a major factor in Mrs Robinson's disgraceful behaviour, that it is not the Pope who is responsible for this (he is quite powerless in the matter – as will his successors be), but Jesus Christ.'

On the same page of that day's *Irish Times* there was a report from Paddy Agnew, its correspondent in Rome. In this report

Mr Agnew wrote: 'Dress code for Vatican audiences has traditionally implied black or dark clothes, with many women still choosing to wear a black veil or mantilla ... Not all women wear veils, while one or two have chosen not to wear dark clothes. Perhaps the most celebrated example was Raisa Gorbachev, wife of the former Soviet president, who word red during a historic 1989 visit. On the question of any alleged offence given by the sombre green worn by President Robinson, a Vatican senior spokesman, Dr Joaquin Navarro-Vals, who was present for the visit, absolutely rejected any suggestion of offence given or taken when asked by *The Irish Times*. Had any form of offence been perceived by the Vatican, it is most unlikely that the next day's Vatican daily, *Osservatore Romano*, would have carried a front-page picture of President Robinson with the Pope in the Apostolic Library.'

However that report could not lessen the venomous sting of Fr O'Hanlon's article. I was appalled by it. So, shortly before the patristic seminar began when I met one of the professors at Maynooth I asked him what he thought of the article by one of his former students in today's paper. And I was horrified to hear that not only had Fr O'Hanlon expressed a personal view of the President in his article but had, according to this professor, articulated the view of the vast majority of priests in Maynooth by doing so. Looking at his smiling approval, I felt sick. It was clear to me that the attack on President Robinson was but a thinly-veiled assault on all women by celibate men who considered themselves to be the true representatives of Jesus Christ – *because they were male*. It was difficult for me to concentrate on the seminar after that. But later on that evening when I thought over that conversation, I felt a sense of frustration and anger at the hierarchy of the Roman Catholic Church. Had they any idea how their sense of election *because they were male* nauseated women like me who, after years of struggling with the challenge of

Christ's words, had finally accepted them as the only stan-
dard by which to try to live, even though I fell far short of
them with every effort? Had they any idea how their sense of
election *because they were male*, so well articulated by Fr
O'Hanlon in his attack on President Robinson, made women
like me want to weep and smash their stupidly proud heads
together before leaving the Roman Catholic Church in protest
at the refusal of so many of its priests and bishops, as well as
the Pope, to read the signs of the times? Had they any idea
how difficult and sometimes impossible they made the effort
to live the words 'Love one another as I have loved you' by
their sheer hardness of heart towards any woman who dared
be herself before man and God? Or before Pope and God, as
President Robinson had?

That day in Maynooth I despaired of ever reaching across the
chasm of sexism within the Roman Catholic Church. And
given that the writer of the newspaper article, Fr O'Hanlon,
was still in his twenties, I felt sick at heart. What kind of
church was the Roman Catholic Church becoming? Where
was the gospel message to be found? Where was the spirit of
Jesus Christ to be found? Did the black suits with the white
collars really represent him and his vision of love?

I thought to forget about it; to put it out of my mind. But
sometimes things that really bother me niggle away at me
even as I sleep, as I discover when I wake up and am somehow driven by something deep inside myself to take action in
some shape or form. In this case, the following morning I got
up, immediately sat down at my desk and wrote my thoughts
about the piece. It was published in *The Irish Times* a few days
later, on 23 April. And because my published response to Fr
O'Hanlon's article in turn provoked a response from someone else which challenged me spiritually and intellectually in
a way that I had never been challenged before, I include it in
full here. But first a word about the title of the published article. *The Irish Times* had given my piece the title 'Incensed by

the Church's attitude to women'. I really liked the pun though it made at least one of my friends groan. But I could almost see the smile on the face of the sub-editor who thought of it. At any rate it made me laugh. What I wrote was the following:

> The attack on the President, Mrs Robinson, by Father David O'Hanlon following her visit to the Vatican is a manifestation of all that is wrong in the Roman Catholic Church. For notwithstanding his attempt to portray her meeting with the Pope as a breach of protocol on 10 counts which he itemises, his article reeks of an attitude towards women which is ingrained in the structures of the institutional church. The fear of women, particularly intelligent women such as the President, is so strong that priests like Father O'Hanlon resort to the age-old tactic of a verbal battering to put her, and through her, all women, in our place – at least in the place they think we should be.

> Does Father O'Hanlon think he expresses a popularly held view concerning the President's encounter with the Pope? Has he no idea that the laity in Ireland has seen through clericalism and its claim to authority during the past few years, as one scandal after another has unfolded?

> The most worrying and shocking aspect of institutional church life in recent years is the willingness of church authorities to foster the distrust of centuries by ordaining young men with a clerical, authoritarian, anti-woman mentality so as to postpone facing the signs of the times. In a recent article in *The Tablet*, Professor Mary McAleese courageously articulated one aspect of the Catholic fear and distrust of women which is unacknowledged by the institutional church. She writes: 'The dynamics of priesthood have altered radically along fault lines some of which have yet to be openly

acknowledged and explored. Women have observed the enormous drain of heterosexual males from the priesthood and the growing phenomenon of gay priests. They are quietly asking what is happening at the core of the call to priesthood that attracts homosexuals in much greater numbers than their population distribution would explain. These questions are not being raised in any homophobic way but are among the raft of questions bubbling to the surface.'

How did the Catholic Church come to this? How could any Christian church come to this? Jesus Christ is such an inspiration: He is the great challenger – to self, to community, to institutions, to society and to the world. He chose to identify himself, not with the ruling priestly caste, but with the marginalised; with sinners, with the poor, with women, with social outcasts, and just about everybody unacceptable to the social, religious and political authorities of the time.

There are those within the institutional church who think Jesus Christ was the first Roman Catholic. In fact, he was a Galilean Jew. Jesus never went to Mass or confession: neither did he insist on his disciples wearing black suits with Roman collars. He was often rebuked by the religious authorities of his time for breaking with tradition. His answer is the great solace to those of us who question the institutional church's current obsession with tradition: 'Why do you break away from the commandment of God for the sake of your tradition?'

My questions to the anti-women elements within the Roman Catholic Church are the following: Can you not see that what is important is the spirit of the gospel and not the tenets of Canon Law or the articles of Vatican protocol? Can you see that what matters is that you live 'in love' and not 'in authority'? Can you not see that Jesus' words 'As you do to the least of these my little ones, you do to me' are the stepping-stones in the here and now, to the way, the truth and the life?

I can see them lining up already, those obedient-to-the letter Catholics who are poised to be offended at what I have written, who are poised with their answer that the church is not for a la carte Catholics; that you take the whole package or ship out. To that I can only wearily answer: though you have worn my faith, and that of other women, threadbare with your exclusive-club mentality, and your self-righteousness, we cannot leave – because there is no way out. Once a Catholic, always a Catholic and all that. If there were a way out, many women would gladly take it, because we are so browned off with the institutional preoccupation with the letter of Canon Law at the expense of the gospel of Jesus Christ that many do want out.

And despite everything, I am hopeful that the spirit of Christ will prevail and herald a new dawn. This hope is fuelled by the witness of courageous priests such as Austin Flannery, David Smith, Eltin Griffin, Michael Hurley, Tom Stack and Bishop John Kirby, who have publicly disassociated themselves from the mentality and sentiments expressed by Father O'Hanlon. With men like these, there is some hope that the spirit of the gospels will flourish.

When you write something out of your system there is a sense of peace and contentment and purification of a kind. At least that is how it is for me. When my article was published I felt cleansed somehow. It was as if the venom and spite which had drenched me on reading Fr O'Hanlon's article was washed off. The reaction of many of my colleagues at Milltown was startling in that it was so positive and I found that very heartening. My family were also immensely sup-portive and that was a great help to me both emotionally insofar as I (perhaps like everyone who publishes something) felt in need of support, and also intellectually, insofar as their judgements are usually sound and I value them highly for that reason. But on the other hand, one of my closest friends was rather appalled at what I had written. All in all however, I felt the peace and contentment that ensues after a catharsis of a deeply personal kind and as far as I was concerned that was my last word on the matter. But little did I know then that a challenge was on the way as a consequence of what I had written; a challenge that would change my world.

The challenge came in the form of a letter to the editor of *The Irish Times* (5/5/1997) in response to my article. It was written by Virginia Kennerley, who I now know to be one of the first women to be ordained a priest of the Church of Ireland, the first woman to be appointed a Canon of that church, and who is generally known by the abbreviated form of her name, Ginnie. She wrote:

> I can line up with almost everything Dr Noreen O'Carroll said in her article headed 'Incensed by the Church's attitude to women'. But I am puzzled by one thing. Faced with the expected rejoinder of the 'obedi-ent-to-the letter Catholics' to her protest, that she can 'take the whole package or ship out', she insists that: 'There is no way out ... Once a Catholic, always a Catholic and all that'.
>
> I wonder could she expand on the 'and all that'? I too admire the 'courageous priests' she mentions, and am privileged to call some of them my friends; and I appreciate that they give her hope. But 'no way out', even for those whose present position is insupportable? In this ecumenical age, and at a time when I understand the Anglican Roman Catholic International Commission's agreement on the Eucharist has at last found some degree of approval in Rome, how can there be 'no way out'? Who has locked the door and thrown away the key?

Please understand that I am not proselytising. Anglicans dread that, and I more than most. But Church of Ireland doors, and Church of Ireland sacraments, are always open to Christians of other denominations seeking the sacramental presence of Christ, whether for one occasion, for longer, or indefinitely. The only condition that may be made is that such guests be baptised Christians and communicants in their own church. Many rank-and-file Catholics around the country accept this invitation on particular occasions, and this gives me hope for a truly ecumenical future. Very few would 'cross the line' to membership on a permanent basis, unless (sometimes in protest at 'Ne Temere' excesses) through marriage; but some have done so, including one who is now a priest of the Church of Ireland. I have no doubt that it took considerable courage.

As I understand it, great courage is needed because membership of the Roman Catholic Church in Ireland has long been not only a matter of faith and family inheritance but a socio-political statement of national identity. Is this why there is 'no way out'? Surely it is not still a case of 'extra ecclesiam (Romanam) nulla salus'?

The Church of Ireland was certainly once seen as 'the Church of the oppressor'; and so it was, arguably up to the time of its disestablishment, nearly 130 years ago. Dr O'Carroll's words confirm something that I have sensed often enough before, that the Church of Ireland (and I acknowledge that there are problems with this nomenclature) is still instinctively seen as somehow alien and even inimical to Irishness, even by many of the most thoughtful and progressive Roman Catholics, despite the increased measure of theological agreement between our churches and the undisputed Irishness of our members, and that by a curious inversion of history it is we who are now ecclesiologically 'beyond the Pale'. (Some people would call that 'karma'!)

If this is indeed so, it is a shame, because we have so much to give each other from the best of each of our traditions. And this country needs the very best that we can find between us.

All good wishes to her, anyway. And may her hopes regarding the magisterium's and the conservatives' attitude to women, as well as mine regarding their attitude to fellow Christians, one day be fulfilled.

I read her letter carefully. Then I read it again. And re-reading it once more, I felt as if Canon Kennerley, in the most elegant way possible, had just lobbed three hand-grenades into my life, leaving me reeling, intellectually and spiritually. In an instant I knew that I had a choice: to pick up the hand grenades and deftly lob them back where they came from and carry on as if nothing had happened. Or I could watch them as they exploded all around me and then set about dealing with the new reality in which I found myself.

The reason I am writing this, of course, is that I did the latter: let the hand-grenades explode and stood there in the middle of it all without attempting to hide or seek shelter of any kind. What is it about conflicts that compels us – some of us at any rate – to stand out in the middle of them and take them on? For myself, I can only say that it has something to do with being persuaded by the insight of Heraclitus, the ancient Greek philosopher who wrote: 'Harmony consists of opposing tension, like that of the bow and the lyre.' In other words, peace and order cannot be pursued as such; rather they *ensue* from conflict, whether that conflict be personal, social or political. In this case the conflict was deeply personal, but for all that embedded in an ecclesiastical context. And I had been unaware of what that conflict was essentially about until I read Ginnie Kennerley's letter.

In my article concerning the church's attitude to women, I had written out of a sense of frustration and incomprehension at the male, celibate hierarchy's attitude to women, exemplified by Fr O'Hanlon's attack on President Robinson. But despite my criticism and rejection of the institutional church in this regard, I was, unknownst to myself, locked into that institution and its claim to be the true expression of the spirit of the gospels. Moreover, in rejecting the institution's *modus operandi*, I saw no alternative to trying to live the gospel message other than as a less-than-gruntled Roman Catholic, staying within the institutional fold but constantly spiritually sapped by its preoccupation with the letter of the law at the expense of the spirit of the gospels.

And I saw no alternative because the only one that presented itself at the level of an idea was that of following the gospel message as an individual and just getting on with life, disregarding any form of community worship at all. Much as that had to commend it as a way to live a good life, it struck me as faintly absurd to think of it as specifically 'Christian'. For it seems to me that to be, to try to be a Christian, of necessity involves some social or community dimension of prayer, worship and action. After all, Jesus Christ began his ministry of spreading the good news by gathering about him special friends. Friendship strikes me as being the core of Christ's relationships with his fellow men and women; he both offered friendship and accepted it freely. The transmission of the message was undertaken by the group of friends; at times, individually it is true, but there was always the group, the community, the little fraternity to return to for companionship and support in both good times and bad. It is also a striking feature of Jesus's friends that their number varies in the different account we have of him and his life. Perhaps this is because each gospel writer wrote from his perspective only and an individual perspective is necessarily limited. Just as we are often surprised to discover (usually at funerals) how many and varied our friends' friends are, so it should not be too surprising to find that Matthew, Mark, Luke and John each had a different picture and knowledge of Jesus' relations with those around him. No matter which gospel account we read, it is clear that the group of friends included both women and men who shared with each other in a social way, not only praying together but dining together in a normal way. So because friendship was so central to Jesus' life and message and the transmission of that message to the whole world, a form of life which attempted to live the spirit of the gospels while ignoring its communal dimension, struck me as a travesty of Christ's teaching. For that reason the phrase which I had heard in primary school, 'once a Catholic, always a Catholic' was perfectly intelligible, in the sense that once one has participated in Christ's love, then it is impossible ever to forget it altogether. It remained perfectly intelligible even when participation in the Catholic Church felt like participation in an institutional shell which had lost the fire that originally gave life to its centre. And like the frantic robin in the fairy story who spent an entire night fanning the embers to keep the flame alive that would give life-giving warmth to the human race, so too did I and many other women expend a great deal of energy, both active and contemplative, in sweeping up the embers and trying to preserve the spark of living flame that alone nourished the life of the institution and its members. And 'there was no way out' as far as I was concerned, because if one ceased to care for the living flame that gives life, then one would die sooner or later. True, it was 'a moral death' I had in mind. But that human beings are endowed with the intelligence to recognise that choices have to be made with regard to how to live which ultimately lead along one of two paths, good or evil, I had no doubt because of the abundance of evidence from both past and present.

But Ginnie Kennerley's letter challenged the assumptions underlying the statement 'There is no way out ... Once a Catholic, always a Catholic and all that' through three questions which blasted great, big, gaping holes in my world – both the carefully constructed intellectual world wherein I justified my faith and participation in the Roman Catholic rites as well as the faith-life through which I expressed my relationship to God. However, those questions are equally relevant to anyone who shares my experience of the Roman Catholic Church. They are:

In this ecumenical age, how can there be no way out? Who has locked the door and thrown away the key?

Is the reason why there is no way out based on the fact that Roman Catholicism is a socio-political statement of national identity?

Is it still a case of 'outside the Roman Catholic Church there is no salvation?' [extra ecclesiam (Romanam) nulla salus?]

To say that these questions embarrassed me is something of an understatement. But my sense of embarrassment was as nothing compared to the sense of shock I got when I read Ginnie's letter. And besides embarrassment and shock, there was also a sense of shame. Even now I do not know if it was an intellectual or spiritual shame at not having asked myself such questions during any of my periods of disillusionment and alienation from the institutional church. Perhaps it was both. But I know that I won't be able to rest easy until I find the answers to her questions – because taken collectively they challenge me to explain to myself 'Why do I remain a Roman Catholic'? And that is the task I have set myself in writing this book.

There is one final point I would like to mention in connection with Canon Kennerley's letter in The Irish Times. And that is, that the few people I mentioned it to reacted by expressing the view that she was 'canvassing' for the Church of Ireland. That, in spite of the fact that she explicitly stated 'Please understand that I am not proselytising'. It never occurred to

me at any stage that she was proselytising and I was astonished by that reaction in others. But I put it down to the fact
that they had not bothered to read her letter carefully. If they
had, they couldn't have missed her three challenging questions. However, a letter in response to Canon Kennerley's
appeared in *The Irish Times* on 14 May from a Fr Edward
Downes. Fr Downes stated bluntly the view that I had heard
expressed from others. In his brief letter he wrote:

> Virginia Kennerley's letter (5/5/97) raises some inter-
> esting questions. What is the difference between ecu-
> menism and recruiting for one's own church? I always
> thought ecumenism meant working within one's own
> church for reform and, so, leading eventually to the
> reunion of all churches. Ecumenism needs lots of
> encouragement in today's climate. It calls for a long-
> term view, rather that a short-term one. A sense of
> 'Rome's difficulties are the other churches' opportuni-
> ties' could inhibit the worthy cause of ecumenism.'

His letter threw me into a further state of confusion and turmoil. There was no doubt, he had a point. And at the same
time, he missed Canon Kennerley's challenge by a mile. I discussed it with the Dean of Theology at the Milltown Institute,
showing him Fr Downes' letter. He chuckled. What of the
Church of England's difficulties being Rome's opportunities,
he wondered, alluding to the fact that married Anglican clergy
who oppose the ordination of women in their own church
continue to be welcomed and ordained by the Roman
Catholic Church. The scales fell from my eyes. Fr Downes'
critique of Canon Kennerley evaporated, but her challenge to
me remained – and still remains.

Having busied myself with everything and anything for the
past couple of months, I find that her challenge is with me at
every moment of my days and nights. Why do I remain in the
Roman Catholic Church when I am so fed up with its treatment of women, with its preoccupation with canon law and

tradition, with its refusal to read the signs of the times? Is it because, as Virginia put it, I have somehow locked myself in and thrown away the key – for whatever perverse reason? Or is it because being a Roman Catholic is a socio-political statement of national identity on my part? Or is it because I secretly believe that outside the Roman Catholic Church, there is no salvation?

It is easy to attempt a brief answer to the second and third questions. I don't think of my religious denomination as a socio-political statement of my identity; nor do I think that all non Roman Catholics are damned, though I need to explore why I hold those views. But it is not so easy to answer the first question. Why do I feel that there is no way out? I have to answer Virginia's questions. And that means discovering why I want to be a Christian as well as how to be a Christian – come what may.

CHAPTER 2

The end of happy times

The strange thing is, when I try to find reasons why I am a Christian and a Roman Catholic Christian at that, I cannot think of any offhand. But I can think of one very good reason for *not* being a Christian or *not* wanting to be one, ever. That reason is anchored in an event that took place many years ago. When it happened there was pain and bewilderment and a sense of having been deceived and betrayed by the church. Anger came later; how much later I have yet to ascertain, but when it came it burned through my life like a wild forest fire, consuming me to begin with and afterwards, anything and anyone associated with the institutional church. And it scorched Christ and God, that anger; it still does at times, and still at times I feel as I felt then: that he deserves it. Would there be all that pain and white-hot anger if I had been brought up in a non-Christian denomination, I sometimes wonder? I shall never know. It is impossible to say what might have been. One has to deal with the reality one finds oneself in.

My reality was fairly ordinary until I was sixteen. I grew up in Tralee, Co Kerry, the second eldest of nine children, five boys and four girls. There was always company, someone to play with, to fight with, to discuss and swop books with; household chores to be done and toddlers and children to care for. There were always toddlers and children. Years later when my youngest brother came to Dublin to college, we sat reminiscing one evening and I was astonished to hear him say that our family was always old. I couldn't believe it. But there were always babies, I said; nappies to change, children to mind, children to find after they ran playing hide and seek in the sandhills in Carrahane. But of course, he didn't experience it that way, being the youngest of nine. He thought we were always old. I suppose it must have looked that way to him, looking up the line at eight older sisters and brothers. It was an interesting lesson in perspective.

But when I look back in time to that awful day, I cannot see the children at all. I can only hear them; hear their excitement as they played with their toys. I wonder if I saw them at all that day, only heard them. It was Christmas Day. Early that morning, very early, the phone rang. Daddy answered it and immediately Hannah and I who shared a room, knew something was wrong. I don't recall getting up but we were up very quickly. Mammy was ashen-faced. Grandmother was gone missing. Her bed had not been slept in. They were going back to the strand to search for her. Then they were gone. I remember asking Hannah, puzzled: 'But why would Grandmother go back for a walk in the strand?' It was a cold, Christmas morning. She would freeze and get wet. I saw her in my mind's eye, alone and lonely, walking along the back road to Carrahane, crying. I knew she would be crying. But when we met her in town the day before, Mammy and I, outside the Crosty Bar, or maybe it was the day before Christmas Eve, she was delighted to see us. We would be going out to her, all of us, on Christmas Day after dinner. She was meeting Kitty, I think, her sister, my grand-aunt, in the Crosty. They always dropped into the Crosty when they came to town. It was owned by cousins of theirs and they were very close and ever since I can remember I recall hearing about meeting so-and-so in the Crosty Bar. It was called after the Crosty Rock, a huge outcrop overlooking the back strands of Barrow and Carrahane. As children we often went there when we were out in Grandmother's.

Some time during the morning Daddy came back to see how we were. There was no sign of Grandmother. They had searched the strand, the fields, the sheds, over the road, but there was no sign of her. Then he went off to join in the search again.

Daddy returned later on. He came in the back door of the kitchen looking white and cold and sad. I was standing over at the sideboard. I think Hannah was by the aga.

'Grandmother?'

He came over and spoke in a low, drained voice. 'The poor woman took her own life'. She had taken a carving-knife and cut her own throat sometime on Christmas night.

The rest of the day is a blur, a blur of images and sounds and smells. Mammy sitting distraught in the kitchen armchair, unreachable in her anguish. May and Mrs Murphy from next door trying to comfort her, lost for words, white-faced, shocked. Daddy wordless; and gone with Mammy, for most of the day, to Grandmother's. The children playing with their toys. Hannah and I and Sean trying to pretend everything was normal for the sake of the younger ones. The smell of the turkey. It was Christmas Day and the turkey was there ready to be cooked and the roast potatoes, and the children had to be fed. I remember Hannah and I struggling with the great big bird, trying to get it in and out of the oven; Hannah knowing about basting it and showing me how to do it. And the smell of it, the smell of the fat as we basted it, and the care we took over the roast potatoes because the children loved them crispy.

Later on, I sat in the sitting-room reading my book, pretending to read it. Sean was there reading his too. We were both reading our books and the children were playing up and down the hall, their excited chatter and fun reaching us even though the record player was on. Rod Stewart came on, singing in that raspy voice of his:

'I am sailing, I am sailing,
home again, across the sea;

I am sailing, stormy waters,
to be near you, to be free.'

The melody was haunting. My eyes were clenched tightly against the tears as I looked down at my book, Rod Stewart's words and music were coming from Grandmother's heart, telling my heart why she did it. There was a rock in my throat and hot salty tears trapped behind my tightly clenched eyes. You couldn't cry in front of the children. They would know something was wrong and it would ruin their Christmas Day.

The funeral was terrible. It was in Ardfert. That day, the skies opened and the rain wept out of the clouds. When we got to Ardfert Church, there were cars and people everywhere. Two of the nuns from our school, Mother Agnes and Sister Aquino, came over to our car. They looked shocked, terribly shocked, and just pressed our hands. The Mass is a blur. I just remember my heart breaking and feeling bewildered, so bewildered. At the graveyard, the rain poured down relentlessly and so did our tears. Auntie Noreen had Hannah and I on each side of her, holding on to us, holding us close. We were in pieces and cried and cried and cried. Afterwards we went home.

I didn't think life would be, or should be, the same ever again. But Daddy said, quite sadly, 'Life goes on'. So it did.

Before we went back to school I met one of my friends and told her that Grandmother had killed herself. She nodded and said yes, she had heard about it. And then she asked if Grandmother was buried in a church graveyard. I said of course she was. And she said that she had heard somewhere that if you committed suicide you were not allowed to be buried in a church graveyard. It was bewildering.

Nobody said anything about it when school started. Not my school-friends; not the nuns; not the teachers; no-one. Perhaps it was just as well. But I don't think so. Because here we were in a school run by religious, with religious symbols on the walls and catechism lessons every day and the grotto in the garden and the May procession, all adoring a God who didn't lift a finger to help Grandmother as she lay dying alone on that dark Christmas night; all adoring a God who was deaf to her tears and pain as she began to cut her throat that Christmas night; all adoring a God, who by all the accounts we were taught by the nuns and the visiting priests over the years, was a merciful and compassionate God who had intervened in history to lead the people out of Egypt and who participated in history in order to save us, and yet all he did was watch as Grandmother killed herself. Christmas was a time of hope they told us; hope came into the world on Christmas Day with the birth of our saviour. But when they all knew that a savage death took place a few miles away on Christmas night, so savage and lonesome that it extinguished all hope, they had no words. No-body said anything.

Now I realise that they probably found it difficult to talk about, that they did not know what to say. But that silence! At sixteen years of age that silence was incomprehensible. It was even like a judgement, as if they all said nothing because they thought we were all tainted somehow, Grandmother and all of us. The silence even made its way into print, in a way. Because Grandmother and Grandfather were fairly well known in the county, the *Kerryman* carried a report of Grandmother's death. It didn't mention suicide though. It said 'death by misadventure'. Those evasive words encapsulated all the stigma surrounding suicide and the family of the one who had died. It was such a shameful death that it could not even be named. And that made the horror all the worse.

Now there is a huge public awareness of suicide in this country, tragically because the numbers of people who have taken their own lives has risen so high that, like the swelling of a river, it has burst its banks and burst into the public domain. I have no doubt that the more public awareness, the greater possibility for treating those who have encountered suicide in their families or among their friends with sensitivity. There are also support groups, I think, which is a good thing too. But one of the things that dismays me most is the name of the association which was set up to study the causes of suicide. Suicidology. The Irish Association of Suicidology. I didn't know whether to laugh or cry when I heard about it first. No doubt there are very good people involved in it, but who in God's name ever thought up the name? It's not as if there aren't enough ologies around. There was only one kind of ology when I was growing up. Codology. Whenever we made an excuse not to do something, such a lame excuse that it was easily seen through my mother used to say: 'Codology!' But Suicidology? It is so American, so Californian, so much part of the wave of therapies and isms and ologies that have flooded the world in recent years that it trivialises the awful death that suicide is.

I couldn't understand how Grandmother could have committed suicide. Or how God could have sat by and watched as she did it. She was very religious in the sense that there was always the rosary in her house at evening-time, and Mass on Sundays and the Stations whenever their turn came around. Even her curses were religious ones. 'Jesus, Mary and Joseph!' she would say when she was amazed by something. It never seemed to matter that it was the night-prayer that got said after every rosary.

'Jesus, Mary and Joseph, I give you my heart and my soul.
Jesus, Mary and Joseph, assist me now in my last agony.
Jesus, Mary and Joseph, may I breathe forth my soul in
peace with you.
Amen.'

But Jesus Mary and Joseph did not have any time for her as she lay dying by her own hand, in her last agony. Why didn't they? If God could intervene in history, as we had been taught, if Jesus was truly compassionate, then why did they not do something? Why did the Virgin Mary appear in all sort of places with bland messages like 'say the rosary' and then not appear at all when Grandmother disappeared into the dark on Christmas night to kill herself, Grandmother who had said rosaries all her life?

We used always say the rosary at home too, though since I was about fourteen I hated the repetition, the mindlessness of it all. But sometime after Grandmother died, we stopped saying it. I am not sure when. There was no discussion about stopping it, no decision taken. It just stopped being said. Life went on without it.

Years later it is striking how the prayers and worship which had formed our lives had so little to offer us in our time of need. And equally striking is the ineptitude of those who had given their lives to Christ, the priests and nuns in our environment, to reach us with any shred of the love that they taught conquers the world. Only the words and raspy voice of Rod Stewart touched my heart and offered words of understanding. Grandmother was sailing across stormy waters to be near Grandfather who had died of a stroke that summer. When she neared him, she would be free. Pop music reached into the heart of my experience and in so doing comforted me. But Roman Catholic Christianity which claimed to be the mystical body, in the here and now, of 'the way, the truth and the life' showed itself to be nothing more than a mystical corpse in the aftermath of Grandmother's suicide.

What did I expect from the church at that time? It is difficult to put one's innermost needs into words. But then, there is no necessity to use a great many words when one alone expresses what was needed and what was so blatantly missing. 'Love'. I don't just mean love for myself or my family. Most of all I wanted some evidence of love for Grandmother, to know that her lifetime of faithfulness to the prayers and worship she had imbibed in the Roman Catholic Church, to the Mystical Body of Christ, was not in vain. Christ said 'I give you a new commandment, that you love one another. Just as I have loved you, you also should love one another. By this everyone will know that you are my disciples, if you have love for one another'. But there was obviously a great lack of love in our world. If there weren't, Grandmother would not have chosen to kill herself and we would not be mourning her now. When Christ was alive he loved very humanly according to the gospel accounts. He *showed* that love and because he showed it, people knew they were loved. He showed it in different ways according to the needs of the moment and the context he found himself in. When Lazarus died, he showed his love for Mary and Martha – and Lazarus – through his tears and grief for the loss of Lazarus his friend, their brother. And so strong was his love for them that he brought Lazarus back to life again. And Lazarus wasn't the only one. He also raised Jairus' daughter from the dead as well as the son of the widow of Nain. In each case he was moved by compassion for them in their grief and he showed it by doing something. So I suppose what I expected from the Roman Catholic Church of which Grandmother and we were members was a manifestation of love of some kind; some indication that those in it really were disciples of Christ. There was an endless trail of grief in the wake of Grandmother's death. But the institutional church was not moved by it at all, that I was aware of; or if it was, it did not make the connection between compassion and the showing of it in the way Christ himself did. But neither was Christ moved by that sea of grief. There was no evidence to suggest that he was. He didn't raise Grandmother from the dead.

Elsewhere in the gospels he is quoted as saying that the greatest kind of love a human being can have for another is to lay down his life for his friend. That is a 'doing something' too. But when he was faced with laying down his own life on the cross, he couldn't bear it. On two accounts we know that he felt totally abandoned crying 'My God, my God, why have you forsaken me?' He, more than anyone, must have *known* how Grandmother felt; how forsaken she felt so that she choose to kill herself. That she did it in the dark of Christmas night only accentuated that sense of forsakenness, the sense of being untouched by our love but even more, the sense of being untouched, completely untouched by the light that was supposed to shine in the darkness, the incarnate love of God. At least, that is what we were taught, that love conquered the world through the birth of Christ. That love changes lives. But what I learned that Christmas was that the failure to love changes lives too. And that not only we humans can fail to love, but that God can fail too. It made a nonsense of 'God is love'.

I cried oceans of tears for Grandmother. I cried because there was a failure of love made manifest that Christmas and I cried because the faith into which Grandmother was born was not enough to sustain her in her hour of need. And I cried because I, and everyone, had failed her; because we did not see her despair with eyes of love; and we should have seen such despair if we had looked with eyes of love. And I cried because Jesus Christ had failed all of us, because he should have brought hope into the world that Christmas-time, as he had when he entered the world two thousand years ago; he should have brought some sign of hope to a woman in torment as she slipped into the darkness with a carving-knife to take her own life; he should have given some sign of love to her; he should have given some sign that he cared, any sign at all that would have restored her faith and hope and love in him and in the world and made her want to live. But he did not, even though he could have done because he was God. And with no sign of light or hope or love of any kind to stay her hand, Grandmother cut her throat with a carving-knife as choirs around the world sang 'Silent night. Holy night. All is calm. All is bright.' Thinking of Grandmother with her blood spilling and flowing unceasingly as she lay dying, the light that entered the world at Christmas-time flickered and died for me, like a candle going out.

CHAPTER 3

Questions and mysteries

'Life goes on'. And it did. But it could never be the same again. For in the same way that a nuclear explosion such as that which occurred in Chernobyl has devastating consequences not only in the short term, but also in the long term, so too does suicide reverberate through the lives of those it touches. There were always the tormenting questions. Tormenting because no matter how much you tried to evade them, or ignore them, or run from them through frantic activity, they reappeared and presented themselves like unwelcome spectres from another world, challenging you to acknowledge their presence. That is not to say that life was devoid of questions before this. It wasn't; it couldn't be. But for the most part they were questions arising from awe and wonder and delight at the way the world was. Like why did birds build their nests in different ways? How did the sea always go in and go out? Who lived here before us? Once I had gone walking in the fields with Grandfather and he picked up a stone and explained about flint to me and how it made fire for people long ago. I was fascinated by it. And some time later, he dropped in home with a book for me with lovely coloured pictures and text called *Great Civilisations of the Past*. It was a wonderland, explaining all about the Egyptians, the Sumerians, the Babylonians and Assyrians, the Phoenicians, the Hebrews, the Minoan Civilisation, the Achaeans, the Greeks, the Etruscans, the Romans, the Mayas, the Aztecs and the Incas. I loved that book. I still have it and opening it always brings me back to that field with the flint and Grandfather's low voice patiently explaining what it was for. And there were other questions too. How did spiders make webs? And how did birds know their way to Africa and back again? Things like that. Even death was a source of wonder, not fear. Not that I had much experience of death then, but whatever experience of it I had didn't frighten me. Now I attribute that to having seen my first corpse when I was a very small child, at what was probably a wake. Round the corner from us there lived an old couple, Jack and Nora Callaghan. When Nora died she was laid out in the front room of their house. There was a black ribbon on their front door. I remember going in to that room. There were a number of people there and Nora was lying on the couch asleep. I knew she was dead because everybody said she was and there was the black ribbon on the front door and that was only put up when someone died, but why didn't she wake up? I couldn't understand how she didn't wake up with all the people talking around her.

Even the questions that surfaced as I grew older were rooted in awe and wonder and delight, though as an adolescent, I had all the answers. That was how I got into such trouble when I was fourteen. There was such a clear-sightedness about the questions that the answers presented themselves with no difficulty whatsoever, accompanied by an unshakeable conviction that they were absolutely right. If God existed, where was he? The nuns said it was a mystery. I said the lack of evidence pointed to the fact that he was a figment of our imagination. He wasn't anywhere. If he was, why didn't he present himself and prove it? And what shape was the Trinity? How could there be three persons in the one God? Questions like that. And aided and abetted by some of my school-friends, we took real delight in eroding the patience of the nuns who taught us so that they had to resort to their big artillery to silence all the opposition: 'It's a mystery'. The world was a mystery. God was a mystery. The Trinity was a mystery. Men and women and children were a mystery. Everything was a mystery. I despised that answer with all the immense passion of a fourteen-year old. It wasn't convincing. And the nuns who repeated it weren't convincing either. You could see that they hadn't a clue; that even the questions baffled them and that they took refuge from them behind pious platitudes which offered security of a kind. I felt so frustrated every time I came up against such a wall of wilful ignorance. For that is how it struck me: wilful ignorance. And the really frustrating part about it all was that the nuns expected me to resort to the security of pious platitudes too; to stop asking questions and accept, because the church said so, that everything was a mystery. My mother had an expression 'There are none so blind as those who do not want to see' and for me it had a valid application here, in their refusal to perceive the nature of the questions or where they were pointing to. And for all of that, I liked the nuns. Even though they were solid walls of rock-like immobility and opacity when it came to questions about the ground of everything, they were peculiarly broadminded about other things. Like sex though it wasn't called sex then; it was called 'the facts of life'; and sports; and wearing make-up properly, not in a tarty way; and being aware of the issues of the day.

Years later I came across an excerpt from the *Upanishads* or Hindu Scriptures written sometime around 800 BC in which a woman named Gargi Vachaknavi, puzzled about the world she finds herself in, asks questions of a Hindu priest or Brahmana named Yajnavalkya concerning the origin of everything. But instead of getting a sympathetic hearing from a fellow inquirer after truth, Gargi exhausts the Brahamana's patience. However rather than admit he does not know, the Brahmana forbids her to ask any more questions, telling her that her head will fall off if she doesn't stop.

Then Gargi Vachaknavi asked

> ' Yajnavalkya ' she said, 'everything here is woven,
> like warp and woof, in water. What then is that in
> which water is woven, like warp and woof?'

'In air, O Gargi,' he replied.
'In what then is air woven, like warp and woof?'
'In the worlds of the sky, O Gargi,' he replied.

Gargi persists with her questioning and drives the priest to
confronting the source of all the phenomena in the world,
including finally, the ecclesiastical order of which he himself
is a member.

'In what then are the worlds of Brahmana woven, like
warp and woof?'
Yajnavalkya said: 'O Gargi, do not ask too much, lest
thy head should fall off. Thou askest too much about a
deity about which we are not to ask too much. Do not
ask too much, O Gargi.'
After that Gargi Vachaknavi held her peace.

I related to this the very first time I read it. At fourteen years
of age, I was Gargi and Gargi was me. Both of us knew,
though neither of us could articulate, that the questions we
were asking were not just any old questions, but rather one
question: the question concerning the ground of reality. And
far from asking this question as if it were simply a mental
problem that had to be solved, there was a sense of being
drawn to ask it by something greater than myself; of being
impelled to ask it by the nature of the reality within which I,
and everyone else, was immersed. And in both our cases,
Gargi's and mine, there was a prohibition placed on our questioning; on her by the Hindu priest, and on me by Roman
Catholic nuns. The fact that the prohibitions were enforced by
two very different traditions from two radically different cultures in two periods separated by almost three thousand
years, only served to highlight the sameness of our experience. The frustration I experienced on being told flatly 'Don't
be so smart, Miss O'Carroll' whenever I touched on the question of the origin of everything would have been transformed
had I been made aware how precious the drive to question is
and how distinctive of human beings it is; transformed into a

conscious source of liberation. It was strange that the nuns who had given up their lives for Christ and who preached his gospel message failed to see the universal significance of one of the most striking gospel phrases: 'The truth will set you free'. They just did not appreciate that force-feeding with empty formulas and articles of faith that were not open to questioning did not produce well-formed Roman Catholic Christians at all, but rather the religious equivalent of well-trained dogs or performing monkeys. It is a tragedy that they were imprisoned in their own tradition is such a way that they could not see that the questioning impulse, far from being the enemy outside the walls, was actually the vital fire at the heart of all religious traditions everywhere. Now of course I know that there were many religious and priests throughout the world at that time who were not only sensitive to critical questioning but actively encouraged it. But I never encountered it when I was at school.

Now I feel sorry for those nuns and all other nuns and priests who not only taught that way, but were themselves taught that way. I hope they found the path to freedom somehow at whatever stage of their lives. It is never to late to find it. All that is required is the willingness to do so; not mental willingness only, but a kind of existential stamina too, because such a voyage of discovery nearly always threatens those around us and life can become rather difficult as a result. No doubt Gargi recovered from the verbal battering she received from the priestly authority of the time. Her kind of persistence usually recovers its form, no matter how long a time it takes to lick her wounds after being quashed. I usually recovered my form too after being told off or put down. And the questioning began again.

But from having lived through the experience of being forbidden to ask certain questions, and from subsequent explorations in every quarter that might shed light on those questions, I discovered that if a prohibition was not placed on questioning the source of reality, then in all likelihood, the very questions themselves would lead to the source. I don't mean to the Roman Catholic version of the source, but rather to the ground of being in whatever manner it manifests itself to the individual who seeks it. One cannot control how the source of reality is going to present itself, or indeed, when it presents itself. The twentieth century philosopher Eric Voegelin has described the chain of questions that are asked in order to discover the source of origin as an 'aetiological chain'. (The Greek word for 'ground' or 'cause' is *aition*). Gargi's series of questions in the Hindu Scriptures are a good example of what an aetiological chain is insofar as they attempt to move through the entire structure of reality. Were she not prohibited from continuing the sequence she would either have to let the questioning go on forever, or to have postulated some source of the reality she found herself in. Her situation is no different from that of any individual at any time and in any culture who rejects what she has been taught because it does not satisfy, either intellectually or spiritually, and attempts to engage personally with the questions which emerge from her life. One aspect of being human means that it is reasonable to ask 'and where did that come from?' The challenge to each individual, deriving from Aristotle, is to consider whether there is an end to the chain of questions, or whether the sequence continues in indefinite progression. According to Aristotle, it was impermissible to let the sequence go on *ad infinitum* because it leaves the question of the rationality of anything up in the air.

An aetiological chain of questions functions like an analytical instrument in the search for meaning. But because it moves through the various strata of reality, rejecting each one in turn as not being the source of everything, it is very much the philosophical equivalent of the *via negativa* of the mystics. It is this awareness of the equivalence of human experience which was so blatantly missing from the religious education which I received. Had I encountered it, perhaps there would have been somewhere to go to find answers to my questions.

But after Grandmother's death, my questions changed. They were different from those I had previously asked. Was life absolutely meaningless? What was the point of adoring a God who wouldn't help you in your darkest hour? In fact, did that not only prove that there was no God? And if there was, what kind of a heartless creature was he? Were we not all dupes? Duped by the church? Duped by priests on Sundays and by nuns at school?

However, it wasn't just the questions that were different after Grandmother's death. The very source of the questions was different too. Before, it was characterised by the experience of wonder and awe at the nature of reality. Now however, it was a kind of blackness, a tormenting spring of ceaseless questions that bubbled over into a stream which gathered momentum and became a river that burst its banks and flooded through my life. But it was a flood that had nowhere to go. If it manifested itself at all, it would be greeted by the stock responses of ' that is a mystery' or 'God is love' or 'Our saviour suffered more than anyone by his death on the cross' and if you didn't accept this way of looking at things, it was because you were smart or lacked faith. And if you lacked faith, it was your own fault because faith was a gift from God, a gratuitous gift from God; and if you lacked it, it was because you had refused the gift.

Small wonder then that when I left school and moved into young adulthood, Christianity just didn't figure at all. If there were questions to ask, they would be directed to another source because by the end of my schooldays I had discovered that Christianity had no answers to offer. At least, not the Roman Catholic Christianity into which I had been baptised. It wasn't as if any major discussion took place once and for all with myself or others about the matter. Neither however, was it a question of lapsing out of laziness or the acquisition of new habits and friends. It was more a single-minded, daily renewed decision with my whole being to search for meaning elsewhere. And the 'elsewhere' for me was philosophy.

CHAPTER 4

Deep is the well of the past

The route into philosophy was not as deliberate or as single-minded as it probably sounds. I wandered into it by following whatever hints and clues came my way which promised answers to the questions I had. But once I found myself on that path of enquiry, I knew that this was a way to the source of knowledge and peace. It is strange how some mysterious force seems to put things our way, things that we need; and more specifically, things that we need for our healing and fulfilment. There is a huge onus on us to recognise what we are given and that moment of recognition is itself imbued with either acceptance or rejection. Life teaches us that acceptance or rejection have to be nurtured daily, otherwise the one can very easily become the other. But looking back, I don't really know whether it was the case that I did not nurture what I was given, or whether I was simply too disturbed at heart by Grandmother's death to be able to nurture anything.

The summer after she died I did the Leaving Certificate and went to France on an exchange scheme thinking it would be good to brush up my French, since I would undoubtedly take it in college in the autumn. I stayed with a family whose daughter was the same age as myself. But within days of my arrival there, I felt desolate. Not homesick only, though there was certainly that, but plain desolate. And for all the family's efforts to be kind and caring, I sank deeper and deeper within myself. I cried desperately on the phone home, wanting to come home. But my return ticket was booked through Tarbes airport; and because this was the airport for Lourdes, there was no possibility of changing my dates because the flights were fully booked throughout the summer season bringing pilgrims to the town.

As it happened, I had visited Lourdes a year and a half earlier, as part of the CLM group. The letters stood for 'Cuairteoirí le Muire' in Irish and 'Christian Leadership Movement' in English. This was a group founded by a priest named Father Leahy and a woman named Mrs Smye from Charleville in Co Cork. The objectives of the group were to bring young people together, both able-bodied and handicapped, to learn to care for each other. The group was established in my school fol- lowing a visit by Fr Leahy and Mrs Smye and the fifth years girls got involved. There were Christmas holidays and sum- mer camps, all with able-bodied and handicapped young people from all over Ireland. But the highlight of the year was Lourdes at Eastertime. My sister Hannah was one of the first in our school to get involved and her reports of the Christmas get-togethers and the Lourdes trip held me enthralled. So I too had joined when I got to fifth year, and had been on Christmas holidays in Clare and Dublin, a summer holiday in Tramore, and had visited Lourdes in the Easter of my fifth year at school, before Grandmother died.

The family I stayed with were some miles from Lourdes, in the Pyrenees, but the mother worked one day a week during the summer season as a voluntary helper at the baths in Lourdes. So when she asked me if I would like to accompany her to Lourdes, I was overjoyed, because by that time CLM had bought a hotel there as a base. I had visited it briefly the previous year and now I intended to find it and see if I could make contact with any of the groups from the holiday camps I had been on.

The CLM hotel was in Rue du Bourg and finding it was a tremendous joy. But even more heartening was the sympathy Mrs Smye had for me when I told her how alienated I felt in France. One of her daughters had been on a exchange scheme

and felt as I did during her stay, so Mrs Smye was very understanding and sympathetic. Immediately she invited me to
stay. The French family were not pleased; in fact they were
terribly put out, but one of the CLM workers who had fluent
French did his best to explain the situation. So from that day I
settled in to life in Lourdes for the best part of the summer. I
was assigned to the dining-room, because in CLM, you either
had someone your own age to care for, or you were part of
either the cleaning, kitchen or dining-room teams. So I just
slotted in where I was told.

There followed some of the happiest weeks of my life. Lots of
people say Lourdes is tacky and so it is if you see only the
souvenir shops and all that commercial side of it. But from
my first visit to the Grotto during the Easter of my fifth year, I
was deeply impressed by the spirit of the place. Now, I was
given the chance to breathe that spirit daily. The really great
moments at Lourdes for me were in the evening, during the
torchlight processions. Then I discovered that, despite all that
had happened, a spark was alive under the ashes of my faith.
Moreover, it wanted to live; and wanting to live, it was
helped to do so by the spirit of the place. After dark every
evening great rivers of light assembled; people holding candles aloft in the darkening night, singing in every language
under the sun yet all joining in the great refrain:

'Ave, Ave, Ave, Maria.'

And sometimes the refrain would be different:

'Laudate, Laudate, Laudate, Maria;
Laudate, Laudate, Laudate, Maria.'

The power that flowed from that river of light was immense
and immensely touching. It was, and remains, one of the
deepest experiences of my life. I felt safe there, as if I had
come home. The light of the world that was extinguished on
Christmas Day the year before was re-kindled in the dark,
here in Lourdes by people from every country in the world. I

was deeply touched to find myself at home in such a diverse community. Some evenings I went by myself to the torchlight processions and instead of joining in, I went to watch from the top of the basilica. I loved that never-ending river of light.

I remember meeting people from all over the world, all of us from different cultures, speaking different languages yet we succeeded in communicating somehow. It was the first time I had ever met so many nationalities all together and it was in a way a real Tower of Babel experience, though in a very positive sense. But since Canon Kennerley posed the question whether being Roman Catholic in Ireland is a socio-political statement of national identity, I have tried to reflect on whether that is the case for me, and if so, when I first experienced it to be so. Those encounters with Roman Catholics from other countries in Lourdes certainly compelled me to reflect on what being a member of the church implied. But the overwhelming experience for me at that time was one of participation in a church which was far richer, more diverse and consequently more exciting than anything I had hitherto know. So my Roman Catholicism, insofar as it could be said to be any kind of statement, was more a statement of having an international identity, though I did not think in those terms at that time. Moreover it was through that sense of being part of an international community, at a time when my faith in God and the church was all but dead, that my faith was rekindled again by an experience of church which was in the very truest sense, the people of God.

Perhaps everything would have been all right if I had been able to stay in Lourdes forever, sustained by the raised voices and candlelight from all over the world. But life isn't like that. You have to move on. So I did, going home eventually and beginning my life as an adult by going to train as a physical education teacher. I had been good at games at school and my dream was to become a P.E. teacher. But I found that I hated everything associated with physical education: the freezing

cold of the swimming pool on winter mornings, the hard
crack of the hockey ball against your shins, and the general
heartiness of it all. There were lectures too, on everything
from motor skills to educational theory, and the only thing I
got from them and remembered subsequently was some
aspects of Plato's philosophy. Around that time I began to
read some of Simone de Beauvoir and Jean-Paul Sartre and
was fascinated by what philosophy had to offer. But it was
only with the vaguest of plans to study it at the university the
following year that I gave up the physical education after a
few months and decided to get a job until the next academic
year began. I went home to do so. But before long, noticing
how withdrawn I was and how out of touch with everything
around me, my father suggested that I talk to someone he
knew, a psychiatrist. I refused. In fact I was terrified. So I left
home, heading for London with practically no money, only
an address at where I might be welcome.

I spent a few weeks in London, an intruder in someone else's
life, but too sunk in the depths of the past to notice. I worked
in a supermarket in the East End for a few days but soon gave
it up and spent my days wandering around the city. I walked
for miles and miles. Eventually the person with whom I
stayed said she was returning to Ireland at Easter by car and
suggested I take the opportunity of the lift to do so too. So I
did and was deposited outside Heuston Station with the
train-fare to Kerry and advised to go home. But I didn't.
Instead I checked into a youth hostel, spending the days wandering the streets and when I got really tired of that, walked
down to Heuston Station and back again. I did that so many
times I lost count. But I quickly learned that you had to keep
moving if you didn't want to be noticed and railway stations
were great places to be anonymous in because there were
always so many people there. I was desperately lonely but
didn't know I was lonely; at least, not in words, because I had
never really been lonely before, certainly not all alone and

lonely. It was an emotionally crippling time. Eventually the money ran out and I had to leave the youth hostel. At that point I began to get really frightened because I did not know where to go or where I could spend the night. I found a phone box in a relatively quiet street and hung around that for a while, thinking I could spend the night there. At least it would be shelter of a kind. But I was too terrified to do so. I went through the phone book under 'Hostels' and wrote down the names of a few of them. At the first one I called on, the door was opened by a middle-aged woman who introduced herself as Sister. She was a nun, though she wore ordinary clothes. I explained that I had no-where to stay and though I had no money, I would get a job and pay her back if she could find room for me there. She looked absolutely shocked, though not at the suggestion as it turned out, but at my plight. She was kindness itself. The hostel was full however. But she gave me the name of another one which was nearby and told me to go there. She said it was very likely they had a place. But I was to return immediately to her if they hadn't and she would help me to find someplace. As it happened, the other hostel too was run by nuns; this time, more traditional ones who wore a habit. But they too were deeply sympathetic and concerned and took me in, even though I had no money. Ever since that time I have always thought of their concern and generosity with astonishment and deep, deep gratitude. If it hadn't been for them, I would have had to sleep on the streets somewhere. Eventually I got a job and I did pay them back. I stayed there for a few weeks, and then moved to the first hostel as soon as they had a vacancy, because it was less expensive than the one that originally took me in. I stayed with those unobtrusive kind nuns for a few months.

By this time, I had made contact with home and my parents were immensely relieved in different ways that I was all right. I cried and cried on the phone the first time I rang. My mother could not persuade me to come home however. I was too ashamed at having hurt them by leaving without telling them and wanted to do something right. If I got a job, they would see that. That is what I hoped. I got a job within days and it was an enormous relief to have somewhere to go each day and to have work to do. Shortly afterwards, my father came to Dublin and we met for lunch and made our peace with each other. It was wonderful to see him. After that the nightmare weeks of traipsing around London and Dublin on my own were over. When I eventually went home for a week-end, the weather was beautiful, and swimming at the slip during a high tide in Fenit, I couldn't understand how I could have felt so terrible about Kerry as to have wanted to leave it forever. But later on, I would discover that the black clouds that had rolled over my head at that time would return time and time again no matter where I was, and eventually they had to be faced because there was no place on earth that you could hide from them.

The job I got was in the office of a clothes shop on the corner of Grafton Street and Johnson's Court. Very early on I saw the entrance to Clarendon Street church from Johnson Court. But I did not go in. It was a very determined decision. Now I don't know why I felt so set against the church and all that it stood for, particularly as I had spent a few life-giving weeks in Lourdes the summer before. But I passed by the church every day, conscious that it was there, and determined to have nothing to do with it. It was as if the spark that had been so carefully nurtured in Lourdes had finally gone out, though when and where I have no idea.

CHAPTER 5

Breakdown

Over a year after Grandmother's death, Kitty killed herself too. She and Grandmother were sisters and lived on adjoining farms; there were only the two of them, and even though they were both married women with children and busy lives, they were great socialisers. There was always laughter when the pair of them were together and Kitty had a great cackling laugh that set everybody around her laughing too. And like Grandmother, she was also a religious woman, observing all the conventions. I remember the stations in her house when we were children. We were all there and all the children and neighbours for miles around, just like Grandmother's stations. It seems like another world now, one where there was only light and sunny days. When Kitty died, I was in Dublin and Hannah told me some weeks afterwards as we walked around Stephen's Green. She had taken some kind of poison, one of the deadly poisons that are used on farms, and drank it. It must have burned her up inside because she was found fully clothed in a bath of cold water, as if she had tried to cool the burning down. I crumbled when I heard it. The horror of it made me shake and cry uncontrollably and in those moments I really thought as if I was actually breaking up. It was as if you could feel yourself fragmenting. But I pulled myself together and we went on, numbed by it.

In the autumn, I started at UCD and began to study English, French and philosophy. There were about five hundred students in the first year philosophy class and a great number of them took it because it had the reputation of being an easy third subject; the one which was dropped at the end of first year, in order to concentrate on two major subjects for the BA. But I choose it because it might provide clues as to why things had turned out the way they did. Years later I was struck by Eric Voegelin's answer to a question about what advice to give students who are searching for light . 'It's not a question of seeing luminous events. There are actually students who will not settle for less than a vision like St Paul's; they are not willing to believe. One needs to get them out of their idiocy somehow and persuade them that the daily tasks are the things one has to do – to live, to have a useful vocation or occupation, found a family, take care of a wife and children, and so on. That all has to be done; that is life and the meaning of life. Beyond that, if they have time enough to go into intellectual and spiritual exploits there is enough literature for them to train on. We are always trained on something … So take it where you get it!' I was intrigued by that perspective, but found it infuriating too. There was a sense in which I was one of those students who would not settle for anything less than a vision like St Paul's. But I do not think that I was unwilling to believe in the truth. It was just that the truth in which I was brought up had failed somehow; it had failed me and all around me and in so doing, it had shown itself to be a failure. The word 'failure' however, does not capture fully the essence of the experience, because deception and betrayal were also part of it. So for that reason, I found that there was a huge gulf between Voegelin's understanding of the starting-point of the individual in search of truth and mine. My starting point was what I referred to earlier when I said that after Grandmother's death, the *source* of my questions was different; it was now a kind of dark, tormenting spring of ceaseless questions that flooded through my life. Whereas before that, it was characterised by the kind of wonder and happiness at life which everyone experiences at the best of times. And because it was so tormenting, the 'normal' things just faded to the margins and the questions deriving from that experience became the driving force of my life. For that reason, it was with a sense of amazement that I read Voegelin's statement that the meaning of life was to be found in having a useful vocation or occupation, in founding a family and taking care of spouse and children and so on. That view certainly seemed to be shared by the vast majority of people, it is true, judging from the regularity with which people got a job, got married, had children and seemed to accommodate whatever burning questions they had into that framework. But I was beyond that, in the sense that there was always the ever-consuming questions to be answered before any peace could be attained. The one thing I agreed with, however, was the statement: 'Take it where you get it!' In other words, take whatever illumination you find, from whatever source. That was what I was doing: rummaging around in literature, poetry, drama, philosophy, everywhere and anywhere, to find some kind of light. At that time, though, I had no idea that philosophy would become my life.

But as things turned out, philosophy in my first year at UCD was immensely disappointing for the most part. In fact it was even boring a lot of the time. There was no connection between the questions which I had and the questions which concerned the philosophers we were taught. The pre-occupations of the early Greek philosophers just did not touch me at all then. Later on, when I re-read the philosophical tradition, keeping an eye on the background of myth which preceded it, it proved to be immensely exciting and the breakthroughs in modes of questioning as well as degrees of insight became apparent. But my formal introduction to philosophy as a first year university student was an experience to be endured rather than the light shining in the darkness that I had expected it to be. In that first year, I threw myself into college life as best I could. Dramsoc proved to be a tremendous conduit for energy as well as a centre of creativity for the most unlikely assortment of people. I loved it. There wasn't much study done during that year as a result. But afterwards I came to see all that immersion in productions and rehearsals and endless cups of coffee discussing plays with the friends I made there as an immense attempt to survive. I don't mean to survive the academic rat-race that Belfield undoubtedly was, but rather to survive in much the same way that a swimmer struggles to keep her head above water as a stormy sea tosses her about like a piece of flotsam.

As time went on, the struggle to survive got more and more difficult and I became one of the lost souls of Belfield. I wasn't the only one. There was a surprisingly significant number of us, each recognisable to the other in that strange, unspoken way that kindred spirits often are. We were the ones who lurked in the alcoves of the upper corridors, sitting smoking cigarettes pretending to look over notes or read a book. We were the ones who avoided the restaurant when it was full because we were so alienated from the noisy buzz at all the other tables that it made our world seem even more awfully solitary than it already was. We were the ones who slipped in to have coffee or lunch in the in-between hours, so that we could slink to the furthest corners and sit at a table alone and feel that we weren't too noticeable because there were always a few others there at that time, only a few tables away, just like ourselves. We knew each other by sight because it was like seeing a mirror of ourselves approaching when we encountered each other's presence in those places. But we never spoke. Why speak when you know what the other one will tell you? 'Life is hell.' Even so, we were a peculiarly com- forting presence to each other in a way. At least you weren't the only one. But you didn't want that kind of comfort. You didn't want to be like those others. You longed with all your heart to be one of the beautiful people, one of those happy, chattering confident students who knew everyone and was always surrounded by a whole crowd of friends – it was magic the way the whole crowd moved together, like a huge shoal of fish – who knew the lecturers and always got their essays in on time, who knew exactly what to study for exams so that the exams held no fear for them. But you were different. You were one of the lost souls of Belfield, one of the ones who sank like a stone in the water.

Sometime in my second year I went to the health centre with a bursting headache, thinking I was going mad. The nurse in attendance looked at me thoughtfully and asked if I would like to see the college psychiatrist. It was the first I had heard of such a service within the college. In fact, he was right there in the health-service section and from that time, I began to see him regularly. Eventually he prescribed some anti-depressant drugs and I took them. It was quite a struggle to continue going to lectures while on them but I did. Finally he suggested that I go into hospital 'for a little rest'. I was horrified and terrified but in a funny sort of way, relieved too. It would be somewhere to crawl away from it all. When I told my parents, they were stunned but immensely supportive. They arranged for me to see another psychiatrist in Tralee, ironically the one my father wanted me to see a few years earlier, just to be sure. She was, then and afterwards, immensely understanding, and supported the decision about hospitalisation which took me first to St Gabriel's in Cabinteely and afterwards to St John of God's.

There were all sorts of people in John of God's. That was one of the things that surprised me most about the place. I had been terrified of going there. It wasn't just fear of being in a mental hospital, though everyone went to great lengths never to call it that, but referred to it as a psychiatric hospital. But if you come from the country as I did, the name 'psychiatric hospital' was really only camouflage for the madhouse or the county home. And everybody knew that only the real hopeless cases went there. If you were anyway all right, you could just take something for your nerves and carry on somehow. So I was terrified of the place before I ever went there and because of that, I was terrified of the people I would meet there. For the first few days, I tried not to meet anyone at all and stayed in my room most of the time. But you had to go out at mealtimes and the first morning I found myself at breakfast-time in the dining-room in my night-dress and dressing gown and slippers, terrified of the other dressing-gowned slippered wrecks of human beings who shared my table. Everybody seemed to be eating All-Bran, either on its own or with Cornflakes and unsteady hands raised spoonfuls of cereal to pale faces, dribbling mouths. No-one spoke; only fear spoke silently between us, telling us that we were afraid of each other. Eventually I got used to it and when I was given my clothes back and moved to the main part of the hospital the sense of amazement increased because so many people seemed so normal somehow. But there was one exception: there was a nun there, a young nun in a habit with a veil, and she cried a great deal. Someone said that there were a few priests there too, drying out, but I don't remember them. But I do remember being absolutely astonished to discover that a nun was there, and that there were priests there too. Priests and nuns weren't supposed to have breakdowns. They had it all figured out. They believed in God and had faith so how could they break down? That is how I saw it then.

That period as a psychiatric patient was an interesting one, though for all the wrong reasons. I assumed it would mean that somebody, some psychiatrist, would help me in the sense of asking about everything and helping me to sift through the threads of it all. But that never happened. What did happen was I got a lot of different types of medication for depression. No doubt it was needed and did some good. But it did not touch me at all. By that I mean it left untouched that aspect of my being that was in turmoil, that still struggled to find light through the darkness of my world. And what I longed for most, what I needed most, was for someone to sit and talk with me heart to heart. I ached silently with the longing to find peace within myself through unlocking my heart to someone who would understand. But it had to be someone who understood the language of the heart. Only such a person could fully enter into my world. Only such a person could empathise with my state of mind and the events that led to my being in John of God's. Only such a person could comprehend, as Pascal said, that the heart sometimes has reasons which the mind cannot understand. But I did not find such a person in St John of God's and, even though I was young and felt absolutely worthless at the time, I had a sense that something was terribly wrong because the only remedy for everything was medication. And you had to take it. The tablets and pills were distributed by two nurses at meal-times and they stood there until you had swallowed yours completely.

By the end of my stay there I knew without any doubt that the inability of the psychiatrists I encountered there to heal the not-physically wounded was intrinsically connected to their inability to see that the mind of the person is not synonymous with the spirit of the person at all. They did not, or would not, see that the mind can only be healed when the spirit is at peace with itself. And in their failure or refusal to perceive that, they treated the mind with medication and electric shock therapy and presumed that these would make a person healed and whole again. So during my time there, I discovered that I had to find another source of healing or remain mentally fragmented for the rest of my life.

In fact, a number of different sources of healing came to me. The most constant one was my parents and my sisters and brothers. They were always there for me. Both Daddy and Mammy had driven with me from Kerry to St Gabriel's hospital where I spent a few weeks before being transferred to St John of God's; and driven home again that night. I was terribly upset at their leaving and so were they. Afterwards, they came to visit me a number of times, making the long journey by train. It wasn't as if they did not have lots of other things to do in their busy lives, and lots of other children to care for.

But they were there for me when I needed them most and for that I will be eternally grateful. Hannah, Sean and Mary were wonderful too. They visited me constantly. It was great to see them because I could be myself with them in a way that I couldn't be with anybody else. At that stage Hannah was working in Cork. Much later she told me that after her first visit, she had started crying the minute she left my room and cried all the way to Cork in the train. I often wonder what kind of a state I was in, to make her cry like that. It is one thing going through the experience. But it must have been a very difficult time for my family.

During those few weeks in St Gabriel's I was constantly cared for by a private nurse named Eithne Tarpey who was a nurse, friend and protector all in one. She had been engaged by my father through a nursing agency on the doctor's advice and she came at eight o'clock every morning and stayed until evening when I was given sleeping tablets that knocked me out in a very short time. As things turned out, she was the only one in that hospital who treated me as a human being in distress, not as an insane creature whom one had to be wary of. During those weeks in St Gabriel's, while she sat by my bed and talked to me and made jigsaws with me and listened to tapes with me, she kept me alive in spirit by her presence and her kindness and her warm, human heart. She was kind and great fun to be with. Sometimes 'kind' sounds like as if a person is a bit of a drip, but from Eithne Tarpey's presence, I learned what it was to be a wholesome human being. She did not speak to me as the suicidal patient; instead, she spoke to the flickering flame of the spirit within and by her presence and with her care and companionship, she fanned the embers, keeping the flame alive.

Later on after I was transferred to St John of God's I asked my sister Mary to let my closest friends know what had happened and they came to visit me too. They were terrific; so supportive, so understanding, and kept me in touch with what was happening in college and amongst the crowd we knew. Two of them, Liam and Ollie, made me laugh a lot too. They were a real pair of jokers and you just couldn't not laugh at their anecdotes and wit and pranks. I probably laughed more on their visits than I did during the whole time I was in the hospital. And Mother Margaret from Loreto Hall where I stayed also came and was gently though unobtrusively supportive. Now, looking back on that time, I am more grateful than words will ever be able to express for the love and care and companionship shown to me at that time by my family and friends. I appreciated their visits very much at the time because I remember one of my greatest fears initially was that I would be abandoned by everybody for being in that state. But I appreciate them all the more with the passage of time. It cannot have been easy for any of them and still they made the effort and came to see me.

Another source of healing revealed itself during the course of my stay. The first intimation of it came from other people, though from specific kinds of persons. For during my stay in John of God's I came to see that there are really only two kinds of people in the world: people who are sensitive to the reality of the human spirit, and people who are not. My time there convinced me that people who are sensitive to the human spirit treated others as unique, mysterious, individual worlds-in-themselves; whereas those who were lacking in such sensitivity treated other human beings as objects-in-the-world, to be used or cared for, or ignored, according to the mood of the moment. However as time passed, I discovered that the line of division between the spiritually sensitive persons and the spiritually insensitive was not to be found in the natural division of the hospital, between the medical staff and the patients, though it was to be found there, exactly there, in many cases. But it was not the case that all of the staff were unaware of the reality of the human spirit whereas all of the patients were sensitive to it. That was not the case. There were those among my fellow-patients who were unfeeling and cold and brutal with other patients; who would, and frequently did, walk all over you, verbally and emotionally. And there were those among the staff who spoke kindly and treated me as a living, vibrant individual world-in-myself. But such staff-members were exceptions and even then, they kept their distance and engaged with you personally for five minutes or fifteen minutes or however long the interaction lasted, as if through a glass wall.

Only once did someone who was part of the psychiatric hospital perceive my real need and point the way towards its fulfilment. However, it was one of the patients, not one of the doctors or nurses, who did that. There was a group of us there, young people, aged between fifteen and twenty two, who got to know each other and who hung around together. One of the group, Billy – the eldest as it happened – was always in good form, always smiling. When I asked him why he was there, he smiled shyly and said happily: 'I gave my girl a baby; that's why I'm here.' I thought he wasn't the full shilling. When I told the others, they nodded; yes, he had told them that story too. We all thought this was hilarious and had a good laugh about it.

Billy came to visit me one evening during the period when I was in the observation ward. It felt frightful, being there, because they took away your clothes the day you arrived and you had to spend the time in your night-dress and dressing-gown. Its striking how undignified you can feel in your night-clothes when you don't want to be in them. That area was also locked, so it felt like a prison or a cage. While I was there, I was in a room opposite which there was a mural of some kind. I didn't pay much heed to it when I arrived, only vaguely noticing the splash of colour. That evening of Billy's visit, the room door was open – the nurses preferred it that way – and Billy was standing in the doorway while I was in the room. He pointed to the mural. 'Do you know what that is?' he asked pointing outwards. I joined him in the doorway, saw the mural and shook my head. 'It is a symbol of love,' he said, smiling shyly. 'Sexual love, mother and child love, and divine love.'

I was rooted to the spot when I heard those words. It was like being struck by lightning. I looked at the mural and saw the connection; saw it with my inner eye, not with the eyes in my head. And for all that, it was there too, in the colours. It was a moment of epiphany, when I knew that everything would be all right somehow. That epiphanic flash was almost extinguished a few days later by the verbal equivalent of being doused with a bucket of water, accompanied by a freezing cold stare. I was again standing in the doorway of my room. This time it was a nurse who was with me. She was with me throughout the day – to keep an eye on me, they said – though nobody else needed keeping an eye on to the extent that they had someone like her on their heels the whole time. I detested her even though she tried to be cheery and friendly. While we were there, one of the doctors passed. He was one of the younger doctors, tall and very good-looking in an intense sort of way. As he approached us, he stopped, and started chatting to the nurse. He did not acknowledge my presence at all. I felt like nothing; felt so horribly ashamed of myself because I was obviously not worth noticing. I felt even worse as their banter turned to flirtation, ignoring me completely. He exuded authority and masculinity and the nurse simpered so much at his attention that I was embarrassed even being there as an onlooker. It was excruciating. It was as if two people were having a flirtatious conversation in the presence of an invisible person. Only I didn't want to be invisible. I wanted to be a person too. Then I heard him drawl: 'Interesting mural, that.' And I heard my own voice say: 'It is a symbol of love.' And as he turned to me in surprise I continued: 'Sexual love, mother and child love, and divine love.' There was a dead silence for a few moments as his stare fixed itself on me as if I were some strange species of creature that he had never seen before. I blushed to the roots of my hair with shame. Then he said, coldly, very coldly: 'Is that so?' And after staring at my scarlet, agonised face for another few seconds, he walked off.

It will stay with me forever, that incident, that scene, those moments which felt like an eternity of shame. It has been with me ever since. Not because I am embarrassed or ashamed of myself now for how I was then; but because I am, to this day, unable to comprehend how someone in a profession such as psychiatry, someone who was dealing with vulnerable people, could be so very cold. But by the time I got out of the observation ward, let alone John of God's, I knew he wasn't the exception. They were all like that, the doctors I met there. The only kindness that I met from any of the staff came from two of the nurses. They talked to you in a kindly way and those acts of kindness shone like a beacon through the coldness of the place.

One of those nurses was a girl who had been in my class at school. I nearly died when we met there and I think she was equally surprised to see me. 'What went wrong, Noreen?' she asked in genuine amazement. But I didn't know. After meeting her, I worried for ages afterwards that everybody would know; everybody at home would know because she would tell them that I was in John of God's. The shame of it.

After some time there I knew that I would have to get out by myself because no-one else would help me do it. There was no interest whatsoever shown by the doctors in whatever had brought someone to the hospital in the first place. I mean in terms of the causes of why you were there. All that was offered was medication and all that was expected was that you continued taking your medication and you would eventually feel better.

As the weeks passed, the sense I had that there was no hope to be found in John of God's increased. And the more I talked to those around me, the clearer it became that many of them

weren't there for the first time at all, but were back for the second, third, and fourth time. One woman, who looked to be in
her mid-thirties, was back for the sixth time. She, more than
anyone, seemed to me to be a picture of my future self, if I
didn't get myself out of this black hole. It filled me with horror. How could I get out? Nothing had changed since I had
arrived, insofar as the source of my anguish was left completely untouched by every psychiatrist I had come into contact with. How could I get out when there was no-one to help
me with that? I felt increasingly desperate and alone despite
the constant noise and bustle all around me.

One day I found myself walking towards the sign marked
'Chapel' and I went in. It was a sombre, dark chapel, with
long pews. There were two other people in there, sitting far
apart from each other. I went into one of the pews and knelt
down. I could feel the tears rising and a great big hot lump
stick in my throat. Through the blur of the tears I begged
silently for help; I screamed silently for help. 'Help me, Lord
God, help me. I want to get out of here and there is no-one to
help me. Please help me to get out of here.' I clenched my
hands tightly trying not to cry out loud. The other two people
would hear. Then I realised that they too were there in the
same broken state as myself, crying for help; silently scream-
ing for help from the invisible God that we longed to be there
because there was no help from anywhere else and if he
wouldn't help us, we were truly lost. I don't know how long I
stayed there crying silently, begging with all my heart for
someone to help me. The more I cried, the more the sanctuary
lamp flickered like a living red flame. It was a long, long time
since I had knelt in a church and asked for help and I sat
down and cried until there were no tears left and I felt quite
exhausted. But then, at the end of all that crying, there came a
kind of peace and a sense that I wasn't alone. I don't mean
because there were two others in the church. The sense I had
of not being alone came from a sense of the sacred being pre-

sent beside me and taking care of me even though I did not understand its ways of caring. It had no specific identity in that I had no sense of the presence of either the Father, the Son or the Holy Spirit being there; just a sense of the sacred presence itself. When I left the church, I felt calm and resolute and knew what I had to do to begin to pick up the fragments of my life.

Shortly afterwards I made an appointment to see the Director of the hospital. Waiting outside his door, I nearly died with nervousness. Once inside, I told him that I was well enough to leave; that I wanted to go back to college and do my exams that summer. He nodded and suggested that I go to lectures every day, from the hospital, and return to the hospital each evening. At that, I thought he was mad. How could I do such a thing? How could you go to Belfield and get the bus to John of God's after lectures without anyone knowing? Everybody would know I was in there. I couldn't bear that. I refused point blank. Eventually he said I could leave in a week or so. And I did.

CHAPTER 6

Lead, Kindly Light

Getting out was the easy part. I had to find my foothold in life all over again. It was difficult. But I tried to do so. I forgot as best I could about what had happened and concentrated on the present. There was study to do and exams to pass. I got on with it. But even though I had turned to God at my lowest ebb in the hospital, I left him behind along with everything else when I left the place. But the one thing I couldn't leave behind were the questions. The following spring was particularly difficult, in the run-up to Easter. More and more I thought about the events of two thousand years ago in an attempt to believe in them somehow. But I could not believe that Christ was the son of God. I don't really know why I wanted to believe so desperately that he was. It may be that if I could believe it, that I might find meaning somehow in Grandmothers' death and Kitty's. At the time, I was doing the H. Dip. teacher training course, and the school had a system of class Masses in place. I attended one with one of my classes in preparation for Good Friday and found myself deeply envious of the students; envious of their confidence in church; envious of the enthusiasm with which they played their guitars and sang folk-songs during the Mass; envious of their trust that, solemn though the crucifixion was, it would be followed by the resurrection of Easter Sunday. I could have been a creature from outer space in the middle of them, I felt so removed from it all.

The blackest weeks of my life followed. I thought things had been pretty black in the aftermath of Grandmother's death and during my time in John of God's but it was as nothing compared to this. I wanted to die too, like Grandmother. I wanted to see myself dying, as she must have done; to watch the blood flowing unceasingly, to see the life-force drip away as I slipped away to the oblivion of death from the living death that life was. I did not have a shred of belief that there would be anything afterwards, just a silent darkness for ever and ever, and I did not care.

But I was fortunate. My parents were there to help me through the darkest times. They said I was 'always welcome home' and they were always there, willing to help me through the times that I had come to know as the black times. There was also the school-chaplain and the school religion teacher who became real soul-friends to me that year. They had both been through their own dark nights in different ways. Both of them were tremendously enthusiastic about the changes in the church since Vatican Two and devoted a good deal of time to devising innovative liturgies for the various classes. I couldn't understand their preoccupation with the Mass and liturgy and to their great credit, they never imposed it on me. But whenever we got together, our conversations were always exciting and meaningful and I looked forward to every moment in their company. It was the chaplain though, who gave me the words to articulate what was locked in my heart. I dropped in to see him one day when I was feeling particularly imprisoned within myself. We talked and sometime during the conversation he quoted words which helped him to live through the dark hours.

> 'Lead, kindly light, amidst the encircling gloom,
> Lead Thou me on!
> The night is dark, and I am far from home –
> Lead Thou me on!
> Keep Thou my feet; I do not ask to see
> The distant scene, – one step enough for me.'

Those words of *Lead, Kindly Light*, John Henry Newman's

great prayer-poem, touched me deeply. On hearing them, it was as if I could actually see the kindly light. It was what I had always wanted to see even when it was shrouded in darkness. But it wasn't just as if I could see it or wanted to see it. Those words were my words; they were the words I didn't know how to say; the words which were hidden in the depths of my heart ever since Christmas Day a few years ago. These were the words of my being lost in the dark and longing for the light, even a little light, enough to guide me one step more along the way of life. Afterwards I searched the library until I found a book on John Henry Newman with the words of this poem in it, copying them down and learning them off by heart. They are still the words of my experience to this day.

While I was rummaging around in the small school library looking for a collection of Newman's that might contain *Lead, Kindly Light*, I came across a book on the Danish philosopher Soren Kierkegaard. It is strange how sometimes you find the book that you really need at just the right time. I knew from the first moment that Kierkegaard had something of tremendous value to offer. I began to read about him and was captivated by his deep honesty, and the fact that despite his sense of darkness and incomprehension, he could cry from the bottom of his heart: 'I want to find a truth which is true for me; to find the idea for which I can live and die.' For Kierkegaard, a person develops as an individual by passing through three stages of existence, which he called the aesthetic, the ethical and the religious stages. But he can pass from one stage to the next only through making a conscious choice; all the time aware that the alternative to making a choice of form of life was to live in a state of *angst*. This could take different forms, such as an impenetrable darkness of spirit, or a frantic engagement in activities of every sort. But at the end of the day, no matter what form it took, it had to be faced and renounced through an act of free choice to live ethically or religiously. And for Kierkegaard, the highest form of life for the individual, in the sense that he becomes truly autonomous, is the one which enables him to affirm himself as an individual before God, not through a choice which can be rationally explained, but by a choice which he likens to making 'a leap in the dark'. However, Kierkegaard's God was not some pantheistic presence or some vague Hegelian spirit but – and this is what I found truly extraordinary coming from the philosopher who was regarded as the father of existentialism – the God-made-man. From reading Kierkegaard's diaries and philosophical works, I knew that he was speaking from experience, not from the perspective of an armchair philosopher or an ivory-tower academic and that conferred the mantle of authority on his words. But there was one statement of his, more than any other, which suggested to me a possible reason for the bleakness of my breakdown and the dreadful period which surrounded it: 'Without God I am too strong for myself, and perhaps in the most agonising of all ways am broken.' So the writings of Kierkegaard became the focus of my enquiry as I set my sights on graduate studies in philosophy.

I discussed all this with the chaplain who knew the works of Kierkegaard and was very encouraging about the direction I wanted to take. He was the first Roman Catholic priest I really got to know as a person and he was light years removed from the stereotyped imaged of the stern cleric which I had held, unknownst to me, until then. Through him, I got to know a number of students in Maynooth who were studying for the priesthood with the Society of Missionaries for Africa. They were a great bunch of guys. Some of them worked with the Samaritans and the Simon Community in their spare time. One day when I told him how meaningless I found life, he said he knew a way where meaning was to be found. 'Where?' I asked. 'Give of yourself' he replied. And that was how, when I went back to Dublin, that I began working with the Simon Community while studying for the MA in philosophy.

CHAPTER 7

Simon

At least, that was how it began. But after a while Simon became my whole life and remained so for about two years. I continued with my studies during that time and came to really enjoy university life, so much so that my undergraduate years seemed like a bad nightmare from which I had awoken. But my life centred around the Simon Community. And though I had joined with the intention of giving of myself, I very soon discovered that I was the recipient of all the richness that Simon was. From the very beginning when I first applied to join, I was aware of its special character and expressed what it meant to me in a little poem I wrote at that time:

Simon is the man they forced
to help you carry your cross.
Simon is a way of life
that taught my eyes to see.

Because that is what it was for me – not an organisation or anything like that – but a way of life that opened my eyes to see the world in all its beauty and tragedy. It was there that I learned what Christ's message was all about when he said 'love one another as I have loved you' even though no-one in Simon preached at you, nor was it religious in any way at all. However the ethos of Simon was unconditional love and when you see and experience that practised – not preached – it leaves an impression that nothing can wipe away.

The first Simon Community was established in London by a Bow Street probation officer named Anton Wallich-Clifford in

1963. During the course of his work, Anton found that a certain percentage of the population were continually in trouble with the law and spent a great portion of their lives in prison. However, when they came out they had nowhere to go, due to various factors such as anti-social behaviour, psychiatric problems, loss of contact with family and friends and so on, and they had to sleep rough, in doorways or in old cars or anywhere they could find peace for a few hours, in all kinds of weather. It was for people such as these that the Simon Community was founded and it spread quickly through the United Kingdom and Ireland. When I joined, it had a number of houses in Dublin, Cork and Dundalk and I began my life as a Simon co-worker in the Sarsfield Quay night shelter. But as I had no lectures on a Thursday I volunteered to work that day also and found myself taken in hand by a remarkable woman named Miriam McCarthy who introduced me to a whole new world, the world of the truly destitute, the absolutely alone, the poor, the broken, the forgotten, the untouchables of Irish life and society. With her and one or two others, we visited prisons including the criminal mental hospital in Dundrum, visited skippers (i.e. places were people had made their home for the night), and did late night soup-runs. These late night soup-runs usually ended by going to the six or seven o'clock Mass in Adam and Eve's in the early morning after our rounds. The first time we went to such a Mass I was astonished to find what I described to Miriam as 'the vegetable man' on the altar, saying Mass. During one of my first days in Sarsfield Quay, a van had driven up and a man – the vegetable man – had hauled sacks of potatoes and other vegetables from the van into the night shelter. Now it turned out that that 'vegetable man' was none other than Father Frank O'Leary, a Franciscan priest and the person who had been instrumental in getting Simon established in Ireland. I hadn't been to mass for a long time before that dawn and yet I was glad to be there, cold and exhausted since I had just driven round the city all night with Miriam who had endless resources of energy. I remember being truly awed to see Frank saying Mass – I think because it was the first time I had ever seen a man live and work amongst the truly broken ones of this world *as one of them* and for all of that, he was a priest. A year before the chaplain at the school where I did the H.Dip. – also named Frank – shattered my perception of the clergy as remote and detached. But now I saw with my own eyes that there was more to the priesthood than masses and baptisms and weddings and funerals, because Frank O'Leary lived what he represented. It was through both Miriam and Frank, each in different ways, that the notion of being a 'witness for Christ' throughout the whole course of one's life began to make sense to me. Miriam was a woman of extraordinary faith which enabled her to live life in an extraordinary way. There was nothing pious about her. And yet she obviously drew her energy and her deep sense of compassion from her faith – her quite traditional faith in the teaching of Christ through the Roman Catholic Church. I admired her from the first for being so deeply practical and spiritual at the same time. She was the kind of woman I wanted to become: kind, sensitive, compassionate, practical, humorous, yet anchored in something of eternal value. The thing about her that astonished me most when we first met was her sense of style. By that I mean not only style of personality, though she had that in abundance, but style of dress. She was striking, flamboyant, distinctive and truly original. She went everywhere in a fur coat. She was impeccably turned out. Once when I remarked on it to her, she laughed delightedly and said why shouldn't these men and women deserve to be met in a fur coat. Sometimes she got a slagging about it from one of the men, but for the most part, they liked her turning up like that and being one of them. She had a tremendous sense of the dignity of everyone and it didn't matter to her if the people she met through Simon were homeless or criminals or alcoholics; as far as she was concerned, they were people who enriched her life. So why shouldn't she look well when she was going to meet them? Before meeting her I associated being a Christian – that is being a Christian woman – with the utmost plainness; no make-up, dull clothes, that kind of thing. It probably has something to do with the virgin or whore paradigm that my religious education inculcated. But Miriam shattered all that. She was the living proof that it was possible to be an attractive, sensual, flesh and blood woman, and still live the spirit of the gospels.

Frank too shattered my perception of what a Christian is, though in the best possible way. He was so ordinary in every way and yet, through his living of the gospel of love, he became truly extraordinary. But then, I suppose Christ was ordinary too in a way. Shortly after joining Simon I asked to become a full-time worker which I did. That entailed living in the night-shelter and sharing in life there to the full. I spent a Christmas there and Frank came and said Mass for us all in the kitchen. The Sarsfield Quay night shelter was as derelict and dilapidated a building as you could find. People said that it had been condemned a long time ago by Dublin Corporation but we were still living in it because there was nowhere else for us to go. For security reasons, no alcohol was allowed in the house, though sometimes the odd bottle was smuggled in or attempted to be smuggled in. But the offender, when caught, was barred for the night, so such occurrences were rare. Most of the Simon residents were men though there were a few women there too. That Christmas, there was a poignant silence in the kitchen as Mass was being said, and I remember a sense of terrible loneliness there too. None of these men and women could ever have envisaged, when they were young, that they would spend their middle years homeless, residents of the Simon night shelter. You could almost feel the loneliness. By then, I had got to know a few of the men and women reasonably well, so knew something of their tragic personal histories. Life was so hard on them. And as for me, I was lonely too, thinking of Christmas Day a few years before, but all the same, I felt as if I was wrapped in the real spirit of Christmas, which was about loving each other and being there for each other, no matter what. I can still see it in my mind's eye, that kitchen, with the bowed heads and the hush, and the still spirit of peace there. And then at the consecration, as Frank was raising up the chalice, a huge gasp, a roar, came from one of the men: 'Jaysus, give us a drop of that wine!' It was a wonderful moment. Frank smiled briefly and continued with the Mass, all of us joining in the responses. Many voices were hoarse from drink and some mumbled and others coughed their way through the Mass. But in a strange way, I saw the infinite dignity and value of each man and woman there. It was palpable. I think that that was the time when Christ's choice – to befriend the poor, the lonely, the broken-hearted, the homeless and the sick – struck me for being the truly extraordinary choice it was. It made the words of Kierkegaard which had made such an impression on me come to life, particularly the words which pointed to what is necessary if one wants to be a Christian in spirit, not in name *'Only a man of will can become a Christian, because only a man of will has a will which can be broken. But a man of will whose will is broken by the unconditioned or by God is a Christian … A Christian is a man of will who no longer wills his own will, but with the passion of his broken will – radically changed – wills the will of another.'*

During the period when I worked with Simon I discovered that somewhere in the deepest reaches of my heart, I wanted to be a Christian; because being a Christian meant loving unconditionally; because only the kind of love that accepted you as you really are, as unconditional love did, could touch the poor and the lonely and the broken-hearted and the homeless and the sick. I experienced that in Simon – not all around me as if I were a spectator looking on at a Christian drama – but I, in my broken-heartedness and loneliness and poverty and sickness, I was touched by that unconditional love shown to me by the men and women there and healed by it. Not healed in the sense that I never again experienced loneliness or sickness or broken-heartedness, because I did; but rather healed in the sense that my being was made whole again. All the aspects of my being which had been fragmented during the preceding years were gathered together in the Simon Community and I was revealed to myself, through the relationships I built up with others, to be a unity of body and mind and spirit. It was that complex unity that was unrecognised by the psychiatrists who had treated me, and yet it was that which was immediately recognised and accepted by the Simon people. So perhaps it is out of a sense of my own need that I became a Christian; my own need to be healed and made whole again and that is certainly true to a huge degree. But there was also the overwhelming desire to be a Christian when I recognised how I could help those who were truly lonely and sick and broken-hearted. Only by trying to live the gospel of love could I do that. Years earlier I had had intimations of that in Lourdes. But then, there was a sense of 'them and us' – in the sense that at Lourdes you were either a helper or handicapped. And there, I was a helper. Helpers were Christians who did good to others. But in Simon, not only at Christmas but at all times, there was a sense of being accepted as yourself, which applied to everyone. And it was through that acceptance of the person of the other that Simon healed. Over the years I have learned of others who went to Simon as I did, to do good and to find meaning in life, only to discover as I did, that we were done to, so to speak; we were given meaning, through being accepted as we were.

Now I think it is probably true to say that if I had not experienced utter desolation myself, as I did in the wake of Grandmother's and Kitty's deaths, I might not have wanted to be a Christian at all because I would have no understanding of the difference unconditional love can make to someone

who is broken, in whatever way. I would have been nominally
a Christian and a Roman Catholic of course, because I was
baptised. But I would not have understood what was meant
by the words 'love one another as I have loved you' if I did
not know myself what it really felt like to be in need of such
love. When you are lost in darkness and a failure and broken
and alone and lonely and homeless, you learn what those
words mean, even if you have never heard those exact words,
because of the powerful need within for a kind word, for
friendship and love, for someone to reach into the abyss of
darkness and loneliness and poverty and be with you there
and help you through. Simon brought me back to life.

It is difficult to convey here the enormous crack there was in
Simon. Re-reading what I have written, it seems as if life there
was terribly serious. It was and it wasn't. It was in the sense
that it was a healing place for whoever was lucky enough to
find their way there. But it wasn't in the sense that no-one
preached about love or anything like that. The Mass on
Christmas Day in the shelter is the only formal piece of religion that I can recall. I call it that – 'a formal piece of religion'
– simply to explain how life in Simon was generally unstruc-
tured as far as religion went. However, it does a deep injustice
to the sense of community which pervaded the kitchen that
Christmas because the Mass was the centre of our attention
and experience. The words 'where two or more are gathered
in my name, I am there among you' came to life that
Christmas Day in Sarsfield Quay and whenever I recall that
scene to mind, I can feel the presence of a love greater than
any of us there, lighting up all our lives and bringing us
together.

But there was one other time during my period as a Simon
worker when formal religion impinged on our reality. It was
in 1979, during the Pope's visit to Ireland. At that time, I was
a full-time worker in the Simon house in Sean McDermott
Street. I knew the Pope was visiting Ireland because the

papers were full of it and there was a great buzz in Sean
McDermott Street because they said that the Pope would stop
and go into the church there. I think the reason given was that
Matt Talbot was buried there. I found the whole thing very
much over the top because the Pope certainly did not figure
in my life in any way at all, but I enjoyed the festive atmosphere. The whole street was decked in bunting; there was
even a little shrine made outside one of the houses on the
footpath, and people congregated in the street hours and
hours before the Pope was due to arrive. The church was said
to be packed to the rafters, with people in it since early morning and the front rows full of old people and sick people
because they would be sure to meet the Pope there when he
went into the church. Those of us in the Simon residence
house prepared our own party for the day. We might as well
get into the spirit of the thing and enjoy ourselves as everybody else seemed to be doing so. We prepared lots of sand-
wiches and cakes and a great big trifle which was thoroughly
laced with brandy. It was one way of having a drink when no
alcohol was allowed in the house and that trifle was enjoyed
by all who got a piece of it. We were joined for the day by a
few other Simon people and finally the word went up that the
Pope was coming up the street, from the north strand end.
The Simon house was one of those old ones with steps up to
the front door and most of us crammed out on to the steps to
get a good view. The street was going wild with cheering and
waving; you would think Elvis Presley or the Beatles were
arriving. The party atmosphere was absolutely infectious so
we stood on the steps cheering and waving too and calling
'Pope John Pa-ul!' when the pope-mobile stopped literally
outside our door. We got a great view. It was a marvellously
happy time. But when the pope-mobile moved off again, a
murmur of disappointment rippled through the crowd
because it kept going. It did not stop at the church at all. The
Pope wasn't going to go in. He didn't. He kept on going.
Afterwards, a whole discussion got underway in our house

about the disappointment of the old and the sick and all the people who had waited in Sean McDermott Street church because for all their waiting, they didn't even get to see him. Some blamed the Pope; others blamed the priests of the parish; others again blamed the organisers of the papal visit. I don't think that argument was ever resolved. Years later I heard that the parish priest of Sean McDermott Street, Father Peter Lemass, was devastated when the Pope didn't stop. He had been given to believe that there would be a papal visit to the church and he felt truly hurt for all those who had thronged the church waiting for him.

Later on, I did a further stint as a full-time worker in the night-shelter. One morning one of the men came to me before he left, with a present. We knew him as The Painter Kelly. I don't know where he got the name and know very little about him other than he was known as a man of the roads who used to turn up in Simon a few times a year, from his wanderings around the country. His particular way of making a living was selling religious objects and pictures especially at country towns on days like Pattern Day. But that morning he came up to me and said 'A present' and gave me a small silver cross with the figure of Christ on it set in a little marble base. I was deeply touched. Then he went off and I never saw him again. But I treasured the cross and it came with me from one country to another when I travelled and lived abroad. During the times when I persisted in trying to live in the light of Christ's teaching, I used to keep it on my desk, or sometimes, on a shelf on my bookcase. But at other times when I had enough of God and decided that I wasn't going to waste any more of my time trying to please him, I used to take the cross and stuff it into a cupboard or behind some books on my bookcase. It was my way of registering my feelings about God to God in some tangible way.

That cross reminds me of The Painter Kelly every time I look at it. I often wonder what became of him or why he chose to spend his life wandering from one place to the next or where he came from. It also reminds me of all the Simon people who gave me so much of themselves, of their warm humanity, of their humour and their experience and wisdom about life. Once I came across a passage from scripture, I think from St Paul but I am not sure, with the phrase 'we are all nomads and strangers' in this world. I found it very evocative, both of that time in Simon and also of my life. But in a way, we are all nomads and strangers, journeying through life as best we can and essentially unknown and unknowable by anyone. However when I think of all those nomads and strangers I met in Simon and in St John of God's and in many other places, I am reminded of how they brought me with them, sustaining me when I was most in need of sustenance, though sometimes I wasn't even aware of it until afterwards. That living memory presents me with the challenge to do the same for others as was done for me; to comfort, sustain and befriend. So in a way, being a nomad and stranger is the form of life which enables me to try to live the gospel message, try-ing to put into practise 'love one another as I have loved you'.

In the last few years I have been at a number of funerals and sometimes the thought of what will happen when I die comes to mind. And for all that I love my family and Kerry, I would like to be buried with the Simon people, in Glasnevin. I think they would understand why I want that. When Frank O'Leary died, he was buried in the Franciscan plot in Glasnevin and after the funeral I spoke for a while with one of his family. He was from Rathmore in Kerry and loved Kerry too, but for all that, I was told, he wanted to be buried in Dublin, with his Franciscan community where he could be near the Simon people he loved. I could understand that.

I learned many valuable lessons from Frank, though he never set out to teach you something. You just learned from him, from how he was with you and with other people. Once, when we were going through a particularly difficult time in

the Sean McDermott Street house, Frank noticed how dispir-
ited I and my fellow worker were and invited us out for a
drink. But it wasn't to any old pub for any old drink. He took
us somewhere neither of us had ever been before, to drink
something we had never drunk. We went to 'The Lord
Edward' and drank Benedictine. It was a great night and we
thoroughly enjoyed Frank's sense of style and went back to
Sean Mac, as we called it, in great spirits.

Another time, we were wakened in the middle of the night
and found John Keaveney, one of the residents, dead in bed.
We called the ambulance and it came and the ambulance men
took John away in a blanket. I can still see them going down
the stairs carrying the blanket between them and we were
silent as we watched. There was something terribly sad and
undignified about it. I talked to Frank about it later and
found he shared my sense of sadness too. John had been
bedridden for some years and needed constant care. But he
could be quite angry and cantankerous at times; then, at other
times, he was completely lacking in energy and totally without joy which was terrible to see. It seemed there was no way
of reaching him and it was obvious that he found life very,
very difficult. But when I talked to Frank about him after his
death, Frank didn't blame life or John; rather he saw what we
in Simon could have done to make John's life more bearable.
And in this instance, Frank saw that the Simon rules were too
rigid and actually made John's life a misery, specifically the
rule about no drink in the house. That was necessary in the
night shelter because the residents there were younger and
more transient, but Sean Mac was a residential house and
John was a resident. He drank all his life; it was the one thing
that he found solace in. So Frank said that we should have
had the cop on to allow him a Baby Power or two in the
evenings. It would have brought him so much comfort. There
was no danger of him becoming violent because with the
gangrene in his legs, he couldn't even walk. But with our
rigid rules, we had made his physical agony even worse by

not allowing him to have a drink. Things would be different for others in that situation from now on. I was awed by Frank's insight and sense of responsibility and compassion for John's tragic life. It made me realise that rules which don't contribute to the well-being of the individual are worthless and should be dispensed with.

I learned a further valuable lesson from Frank which I have never forgotten. At some stage I was elected to the Executive Committee of Dublin Simon and that entailed attending committee meetings every three weeks and ensuring that all organisational details to do with the houses were attended to. I threw myself whole heartedly into that aspect of things from the beginning and it gave me a focus on another way of making a contribution. But as the summer neared so too did my MA exams and the deadline for the submission of my minor thesis. I had studied on and off while I was involved with Simon, but faced a mountain of work yet to be done if I was to get my degree. So I began skipping committee meetings. At first I phoned in my apologies, then after a while, just presumed that the committee would realise that my examinations had first call on my time so didn't bother to phone. Some weeks before the next AGM I had a furiously angry letter from Frank. He told me that I had failed those who had elected me and demanded my resignation from the committee. Even though I was shocked by the obviously angry tone of his letter, I knew immediately that he was right and felt deeply, deeply ashamed of myself. I resigned and wrote to him. Within a couple of weeks I had a lovely letter from him. He accepted my resignation of course, but he apologised sincerely for the stinker he had written me. Again I was awestruck by the sheer magnitude of his character. He was one of the greatest men I have met. Afterwards, I am glad to say, we remained friends.

Simon changed my life in many ways. One such was that I met someone there who first became a friend, then a boyfriend, and then asked me to marry him. I said yes. Life was wonderful. He was from Finland. So after finishing the MA and after much too-ing and fro-ing by the pair of us between the two countries I went to Finland.

CHAPTER 8

Northern lights

I loved Finland. It is a beautiful country of forests and lakes, with freezing cold winters of short, dark days and beautiful summers of twenty-four hours daylight and the midnight sun. In Lapland in northern Finland the night sky often displays the beautiful northern lights which are quite spectacular. It was my good fortune to obtain a Finnish Government Scholarship and I planned to do postgraduate studies in philosophy there. I lived in a student residence along with students from all over the world and it was my first real exposure to a plurality of cultures and to those of all faiths and none. The first few months were tough because I had undertaken an intensive course in Finnish which meant full days of classwork with lots of homework to do in the evenings. During this time it became clear to me that as a couple planning to marry and spend our lives together, we were all wrong for each other. So we broke up. It was a very difficult thing to do since there was no row and no reason why we should break up, other than the sense that we were wrong for each other somehow. All in all it was quite a heart-breaking time. I dealt with it as best I could by studying for long hours and this assuaged the pain that accompanied the realisation of broken plans and an uncertain future. However there was a social programme attached to the scholarship and during the months that followed I made some wonderful friends. We had some terrific times together travelling to Estonia; going on a skiing holiday in Lapland and a cycling holiday in the Aland Islands between Finland and Sweden. That year in Helsinki turned out to be among the happiest of my life.

It was also a time when I experienced quite acutely the need to worship God as part of a community. I felt strangely restless whenever I wasn't studying or at lectures or doing something and each evening I used to look at The Painter Kelly's cross on my bookshelf, knowing that the restlessness was connected with it in some way. I prayed; *Lead, Kindly Light* was my prayer, but still the gnawing sense of restlessness continued. At some point it dawned on me that what I needed to assuage that restlessness was to go to Mass. I found out where the Catholic church was and went the following Sunday. It was right across Helsinki from where I was staying and took a journey by bus and tram to get there. But when I got there I felt as if I had arrived home. The church was beautiful. Besides, it was not too big, so you felt sufficiently anonymous and not too small, so you felt part of the celebration. I felt at peace there and went there regularly throughout my scholarship year.

Finland is mostly a Lutheran country so I passed quite a number of Lutheran churches on my way to Mass each Sunday. It did occur to me a few times that it would have been easier to go to one of those which was nearer, but I never did. And that was not because I had never been to a Lutheran service before; I had. But even though the service was quite beautiful and I didn't see any huge difference between it and Mass, still there was something missing for me. It is difficult to put into words what precisely that was. It wasn't the fact that the service was conducted in Finnish, because so too was the Mass. All I know is that I felt at home at the Mass and was able to participate in it in a quite natural way. No doubt, familiarity with the parts of the Mass and the various prayers and responses contributed hugely to that sense of feeling at home. But it wasn't just familiarity. It was as if my Catholic upbringing and education had given me an alphabet and a language through which I could express my sense of the sacred and my experience of the presence – and sometimes the absence – of God in my life and in the world. Just as

English is my mother-tongue and the language through which I communicate with others in the way that is most natural to me, so too Roman Catholicism is the language through which I articulate my experience and communicate with God in the way that is most natural to me. And just as I had learned other languages but found myself truly at home in one only, so too I had participated in other religious ceremonies, but found myself truly at home only in one. My experience since that time has borne this out, all the more so since I have prayed in mosques and synagogues, orthodox churches as well as various other Christian denominations.

Ever since Ginnie Kennerley posed her three questions, I have reflected a great deal on them. The first one challenged me to state why I remain a Roman Catholic to this day, especially when some of its practises seem to me to be blatantly unjust. Moreover, to explain why, in this ecumenical age, there is no way out? To explain who has locked the door and thrown away the key? The challenge inherent in that sequence of questions was the catalyst for recovering the memory of my own personal need for what the gospel message offers: unconditional love. And with that recovery, there was also a restoration of a kind; the restoration of the reason why I want to be a Christian. That is, to try to give what I had been given, which was unconditional love. But those questions also compelled me to focus on the medium through which I live out my Christianity because of the suggestion that in this ecumenical age no-one need feel trapped within the Roman Catholic Church or in any other church for that matter. The implication of this suggestion is that if certain features of church discipline, law and traditions are sufficiently irksome or burdensome to you, then you could shop around and find another Christian church to worship in instead. The only way I can try to answer that aspect of her question is to retrace my steps to the point when I, as an adult, identified my need and desire to worship God as part of a community, as I did in Finland. And having done that I have discovered that changing one's religious denomination is not quite like changing one's tennis club. I am a Christian in the only way I know how to be: as a Roman Catholic. I could no more swop the 'medium' of my Christian expression because certain aspects of it irk me than I could swop my language for another one and tell myself that I can *be myself* within it. I would just be fooling myself. It probably isn't a very satisfactory answer to her questions. But it is my answer.

The second question she posed, 'Is the reason there is no way out based on the fact that Roman Catholicism is a socio-political statement of national identity?' also recalls for me my time in Finland. Coming down from communion on one of my first Sundays at Mass, my eyes met those of one of the students I knew by sight but had never met. He gave me a nod of recognition. The following Sunday he was there again and we met after mass and got talking. He was one of the scholarship students from Switzerland, living in the same residence as I. It was quite a surprise to discover that another student had travelled from Antti Korpintie where we lived. But during the following weeks quite a number of us from a variety of different countries met up at Mass, each one having made his or her own way there quietly and privately and each one as surprised as we had been when we met there. And just as I had experienced a sense of belonging to an international community when I had been in Lourdes years earlier, so too did I experience my Roman Catholicism as a kind of statement of international identity when I was in Finland. Given the undeniable facts of Irish history and the contemporary political situation, I can understand why Ginnie stated that she considered membership of the Roman Catholic Church in Ireland to be not only a matter of faith and family inheritance, but a socio-political statement of national identity. However, I can only say that in my experience such membership was in fact the opposite: not a socio-political statement of national identity at all, but rather a kind of spiritual statement of inter-national identity. Again, probably not a very satisfactory answer to her question, but it is the only answer I can give from the depths of my experience.

In May of this year, a few weeks after the publication of Ginnie's letter, Doctor Noel Browne, a former Minister for Health, died. A number of articles appeared in the newspapers reviewing his life and career and paying tribute to him for his contribution to Irish political and public life. In an article in the *Sunday Independent* (25 May 1997) by Professor John A. Murphy, Emeritus Professor of Irish History at UCC, the following description of Dr Browne by Professor Murphy struck me particularly: 'The truth is that he was a visionary, an unhappy warrior, whose tortuous odyssey through so many parties and organisations was a futile attempt to discover the political mechanism which could make his vision a reality.' It struck me very strongly because in the immediate aftermath of Ginnie's letter, I had considered whether the more honest course of action for me to take would be to resign, somehow, my membership of the Roman Catholic Church, and become a member of another church such as the Church of Ireland, where issues such as the status of women within a Christian community, which bothered me particularly, were resolved in a way that I found admirable. Also to be considered was the fact that I had been told by some other Roman Catholics that if you weren't one hundred percent loyal to the church that you weren't really a Roman Catholic at all, so why didn't you leave? However Professor Murphy's description of Dr Browne as someone whose life was a 'tortuous odyssey' in search of the political party or organisation which had inbuilt in it the political mechanism to make his vision a reality, threw into sharp relief a distinctive similarity between the political and spiritual spheres. On the one hand, there was the situation of someone, like Dr Browne, who was seeking a political organisation that was so structurally perfect that it would enable his political vision to become a reality. And on the other hand there was the situation of those who were seeking a spiritual organisation that was so structurally perfect that it would enable a particular spiritual vision to become a reality. Whether political or spiritual, there were those who sought nothing less than absolute perfection and when they didn't find it, moved to another party or organisation where they thought it might be found. The scene has its comic aspects. However, being reminded of Dr Noel Browne's tortuous odyssey was quite a sobering experience because anything I read by him, such as his 1986 autobiography *Against The Tide* and his occasional letters to *The Irish Times* struck me as being bitter and unforgiving in their harshness. I felt sorry for him, to have attained old age with so little obvious joy or sense of thanks for those whom he encountered, and to have to live with himself in such bitterness of heart. I did not want to end up like that.

That description of Dr Browne's tortuous odyssey from one political party to another in search of perfection was like a bucket of cold water: it woke me up to the nature of reality as it is. There is no perfection in this world in any shape or form; no perfect political mechanisms and structures; no perfect ecclesiastical mechanisms or structures, nor indeed, any kind of perfection at all. Anyone who thinks there is, and goes in search of it, thinking that if only she could find it, everything would be just fine, is only deluding herself. Furthermore, coming as it did at around the same time as Ginnie's challenging questions, it helped dispel the dilemma I experienced at being out of step with official church teaching on matters such as the ordination of women. I genuinely and sincerely believe that the official church teaching which opposes the ordination of women is based on a particularly narrow interpretation of scriptural texts and the context within which they were written. The church genuinely and sincerely believes that its interpretation is the correct one. There are those who say that if you don't accept church teaching, you should leave. But neither they, nor I, nor the church, are perfect. Yet the Roman Catholic Church has given me the alphabet and language through which I communicate with God. That is precious to me; far more valuable than any disagreement over interpretations of scripture, or disciplinary matters or to what extent it is bound by tradition. Besides, I am aware that many other people remain members of the church because of what is precious within it, despite their sense of grievance and frustration at much of its shortcomings. So it seems to me that those orthodox Roman Catholics who ask us to leave when we disagree or dissent with some aspect or other of church law should give more time and reflection to the nature of their request. It implies that they consider adherence to the letter of the law to be preferable to living in relationship with God through the means that he has placed at each individual's disposal. Christ asked his Father 'that they may be one'. This seems to me to be the crux of the problem, that is, the problem of what constitutes a Christian within the Roman Catholic Church. However, unity is one thing. Uniformity is quite another. It strikes me that Christ's primary concern was unity, oneness with him and through him, with the Father; not uniformity. His own immediate choice of followers is sufficiently diverse in terms of temperament, personality, style and social status to suggest that he found diversity a healthy, life-giving force.

Ginnie's third question also brought to mind my time in Finland. She asked: Is it still a case of 'outside the Roman Catholic Church there is no salvation?' [*extra ecclesiam (Romanam) nulla salus?*] Is that why one is reluctant to leave the church? It reminded me of my first encounter with non-Christians. It was at one of the student parties in Helsinki, when I was introduced to one of the Chinese students. As I didn't quite hear his name I said 'I'm sorry; I didn't catch your Christian name'. And he answered, very politely, 'I

don't have a Christian name.' Looking at his pleasant, smiling face the penny dropped for me. He wasn't a Christian. I
thought of him when I read that third question and of the
many other students there who were Jews, Muslims, Hindus,
Buddhists, atheists, agnostics and any and everything but a
Roman Catholic Christian. Where did they fit in within the
Roman Catholic perspective on salvation?

However at that time I had another more immediately press-
ing matter to attend to. Much and all as I loved Finland and
thoroughly enjoyed that scholarship year, I still had not
found a topic that I wanted to research for a doctoral disserta-
tion. I read a good deal in the field of philosophy of language
thinking that it might lie there. But I didn't find anything that
I wanted to spend a few years of my life on. The graduate
seminars were devoted almost exclusively to logic and that
didn't interest me sufficiently either. But as the year pro-
gressed I remembered something that had been touched on
when I was at UCD. There was something there that I wanted
to work on. I tried to formulate what it was and after doing so
sent it to someone in the philosophy department in UCD who
I knew would be of assistance in that area. After returning to
Dublin I intended working for a doctorate in philosophy. At
that time I had no idea that the research I would eventually
do would have any relevance to, or connection with, questions such as those Ginnie asked, particularly the third one;
nor that it would enable me to answer it in a way which is
more or less adequate, to myself that is. Whether she considers it to be adequate is another question of course. But as
things turned out, beginning the doctorate did not happen
for another year. After a few weeks at home in Ireland, I found
myself working in Spain in a school reputed to be run by Opus
Dei.

CHAPTER 9

Diversion

Going to Spain had never figured in my plans. But demoralisation can have a huge effect on the way you think and the directions you take in life. In my case the demoralisation came as a result of unemployment. When I returned from Finland I set about looking for a job because I would need to live in order to do a doctorate. But although I did a few interviews for teaching positions, I had no luck. In some cases, the interview process seemed to be only a formality, something to be gone through to suit the law as the job was already gone to someone who had been working within the school for some period of time. It was immensely frustrating. But more than the frustration was the dissipation of any sense of self-worth. I really felt quite useless. Then an advertisement appeared in *The Irish Times* looking for two teachers of English to work in Spain, starting immediately. I had taught English for a few months in a language-school in Helsinki prior to taking up my scholarship so I had some experience in that area. I answered the ad, got an interview the following day, and discovered that the job entailed working in a Spanish boarding school named Colegio Izarra which was situated in the Basque region. It was an unusual school in that there was a large campus with both a boy's and girl's boarding-school, but the buildings were quite separate and the education was not co-educational in any way. Two teachers of English were needed, one for each school. The salary was quite good and comparable to that paid in Irish schools so it sounded like an interesting proposition. Although there were a considerable number of replies to the ad, the school wanted teachers who had some experience of living and working abroad so I was offered one of the jobs. The other one went to an Irish girl who had also lived abroad for a number of years and we met for the first time at Dublin airport three days later, en route for Spain. I was very excited about the prospect of a year in Spain. It was no fun being unemployed in Ireland. The doctorate could wait. So I set off in high spirits, as did Veronica the other girl who was going to teach at the school with me.

We were flown to Madrid on a one-way ticket which was paid for by our new employers. Then we took a connecting flight to Vitoria, the principal town of the Basque region and from there driven about twenty miles or so into the country. When we had taken the jobs we were told that there would be accomodation provided in the boarding school. However, Veronica had lived and worked in a boarding school in Switzerland so knew how claustrophobic this could be. So she suggested that we look for a flat and we discussed this with our employer on the plane to Spain and he said it was no problem, that we could move out after we found our feet. It was late at night when we arrived and all I remembering noticing on arrival was the sumptuousness of the place, marble floors and that kind of thing. Our rooms however were quite Spartan. In daylight it was clear that we were miles from anywhere, deep in the Basque countryside which was very beautiful, quite hilly with lots of trees everywhere. We were assigned classes and began work. After a day or two, Veronica and I decided to explore the area and to find the nearest village which we were told was about two or three miles away. All of the single teachers like ourselves lived in the boarding school, but none of them was interested in coming with us to the village. Those who were married travelled in each day either by car or by bus along with the day pupils from around the area. We were advised by some of the other teachers in the school that it would be better not to go to the village, which we found a bit peculiar. But since the school was quite palatial, we attributed this reluctance to a certain kind of snobbery: i.e., big school on the hill does not associate with village, that kind of thing. We walked to the village, found a bar and went in for a drink. It was the kind of place which rarely, if ever, saw any tourists and we were an obvious source of curiosity in the bar and the local grocery shop where we went to buy some odds and ends.

Living and working in the boarding school was actually quite claustrophobic. Our rooms were in the same corridors as the pupils and there was no sense of privacy at all because even when you were in your room, there was the constant buzz from the girls in the rooms on either side. So within a week, we began making plans to move out, and after work used to walk to the village, sometimes staying there for supper and returning to the school around ten o'clock. This was discouraged, first by Carmen, the Spanish woman who taught English and who was a sort of supervisor to us, and afterwards by the other teachers who we tried to persuade to join us for a drink some evening in the village. Carmen was actually a very nice woman but clearly found our desire to get out of the school after work to be quite bizarre. We were there to be mentors to the girls, we were told. The school principal didn't like our going off after class hours. So we shouldn't do it. We discussed this among ourselves and decided that we had come here to work, not to be incarcerated, so we were going to have some kind of a social life and move into a flat in Vitoria as soon as it became possible for us to do so. The thing is, we had no way of going to Vitoria, and even though we asked some of the teachers with cars who travelled to and from the school each day to give us a lift, nobody did. They always had some excuse; either they were not going to Vitoria that day, or they had a full car or something. So our plans to find a flat were very much at the plan stage.

On one of those first days when we went to the village after work, we met some teachers from the local primary school in one of the bars who spoke fluent English. When they heard

that we were working in Colegio Izarra, a conversation
ensued in rapid Spanish and the words 'Opus Dei' were mentioned. Reverting to English they cautiously inquired if we
knew who we were working for. So we told them how we
came to be there. Did we not know that the school was run by
Opus Dei? they asked. We were both a bit puzzled. Who or
what was Opus Dei? The name was vaguely familiar but neither of us knew very much about it. I thought it had something to do with some religious group but that was about all.
They told us that Opus Dei was an extremely secretive, con-
servative, right-wing Spanish organisation and that it had
something to do with the University of Navarra and had
schools throughout Spain. Ours was one of them. There was
some controversy in Spain at that time about Opus Dei and
its dealings with a building firm named Rumasa which was
also supposed to have something to do with our school. We
should get out of there as soon as possible, they told us; Opus
Dei had a reputation for brain-washing people and we would
not be able to remain immune to it if we continued living in
the school.

We discussed all this on the way back to the school. Although
what we had been told seemed to be over the top in many
ways, it made sense too. There was the insistence on us living
in, with no outside contact; of being mentors to the girls; and
there was the undeniable wealth of the school. We started
asking questions of the other teachers who initially looked
quite astonished, but immediately clammed up or changed
the subject. We got no information from them. But one day in
class some of my own pupils asked me if I knew when I left
Irlanda to work in Spain that I was coming to an Opus Dei
school? I asked them how they knew it was run by Opus Dei
only to learn that some of their parents were members of the
organisation.

We began to feel fed up with the general air of secrecy whenever we asked anything about Opus Dei. But then we discov-

ered that there was one teacher who was prepared to speak out. It was one of the male teachers. From the beginning, I had been assigned to teach in the boys' school and Veronica in the girls' school and we usually had lunch with the other female teachers in the dining-room of the girls' school. But after about two weeks, having heard the stories about Opus Dei, we decided that we wanted to live normal lives; that we hadn't come there to live like contemplative nuns so we began to go the dining-room in the boys' school for lunch. This caused quite a furore in both schools. The female teachers were quite appalled; you would think we were doing something terribly promiscuous by dining with the male teachers and they, for their part, welcomed us though they seemed hugely amused that we dared to dine with them. One day when we asked them if the school was run by Opus Dei one of the older teachers let out a bear-like roar, 'Not Opus Dei! Opus Diable! Opus Diable!' We couldn't figure out what he was doing there if that was his opinion, but it turned out that some of the teachers were not members, as he wasn't; they only worked there. However, it became clear over the next few weeks that though that was his privately held view, he did not share it with the school authorities and complied with the school discipline in all respects. But as he was married, he could come and go every day, do his job and collect his salary at the end of the month without any intrusion on his personal or social life, unlike the pair of us.

There were other features of our behaviour which clearly irked the school authorities. One was my running. While in Helsinki I had rediscovered my love of sports and had become quite fit through running and skiing. While in Lapland I had completed a number of cross-country ski-trips with a group of friends. It was a magnificent experience, being miles and miles from anywhere and seeing wild reindeer roaming in the snow. And in the spring every year in Helsinki it was the tradition to hold a ten kilometre road race called Akateeminen Vartti, which roughly translates as the

'Academic Quarter', which is a reference to the fifteen minutes break that there usually was between lectures. The custom was for various teams of ten runners each to run a relay race around Helsinki and to complete it in that time. There were always over a hundred teams or more in the race and it was quite a spectacle and great fun, though each team took it quite seriously and wanted to win. During my time there I was on the scholarship students' relay team; the only female student on the team, with my team-mates coming from various countries including Russia, Italy, Israel, Norway, America, Switzerland and Austria. Quite a few of my friends that year were keen runners and we trained together regularly, running in the forest where we lived. When I returned home that summer I had continued running, despite the demoralisation of the job interviews, so was keen to maintain my level of fitness while in Spain. But from the very first, it was clear that the school authorities had a peculiar attitude to girls' and womens' participation in any kind of sports. There were tennis courts in the school and some of the pupils were very good players. But whereas the boys were allowed to wear the traditional tennis whites, the girls weren't. They had to wear track suit trousers. Tennis skirts were regarded as indecent. This struck both Veronica and I as crazy particularly as the weather, even in the early autumn, was quite sweltering. But that was the rule. So the first time I decided to go for a run, wearing the usual runner's gear of shorts and top, I scandalised everybody. But I didn't care. If I didn't run, I would lose my fitness. It didn't seem to matter to anybody that I ran at seven in the morning when there were very few people moving about; it still caused a scandal. I used to do a few miles through the countryside before work, and looking back on it now, I think it kept me sane while I was in that school.

Another cause for scandal was Veronica's and my determination to get out of the school and go to Vitoria to look for a flat. We hitched. On one such excursion the school bus passed us by on the road and we could see the look of incredulity on the faces of the teachers who were in it. That too was relayed back to the school authorities and displeased them greatly.

It was actually impossible to discover who was really in charge at the school. The ostensible principals of the boys' and girls' schools were a husband and wife team who were always impeccably dressed. Moreover the wife was, as the saying goes, dripping in gold. She had a huge collection of jewellery. Even their little boy who was about seven and a pupil in the school, wore a huge gold ring. Apart from shaking our hands and welcoming us on our first day at the school, they never spoke to us. This no doubt was due to the fact that they had no English. So their thoughts and wishes were communicated through the other teachers, usually Carmen. But while they were the effective heads of each school, there was a priest there too who seemed to have considerable authority. He used to teach religious education but he quite obviously had some administrative role as well. He was very traditional in dress, wearing the clerical black suit and roman collar, and like the principals, he too never spoke with us. But we picked up from the other teachers that he was the real power there. We were quite wary of him because although he never spoke with us, he used to force his face into a smile and flash his teeth at us whenever we met him. We nicknamed him 'the Gnasher' from the way he used to gnash his teeth into that fake smile.

For a few weeks everything seemed fine. It looked to us as if we wouldn't be able to go and look for a flat until the Christmas holidays so we resigned ourselves to living in the school until then. We did our work well, I think. Both of us gave the necessary time to class preparation and the correction of homework, and we participated in any school activities which asked for our presence. On Sundays we went to Mass along with all the other girls and female teachers in the school. Mass too was segregated in that each school had its own. It was quite formal, as everything in the school was. In fact, it was quite a turn off. For even though it was supposed to be a school with a religious ethos, there was very little sense of genuine human warmth there. And for all that there was great emphasis on God and prayers, there was very little sense of the sacred there, in the way that I had experienced it at various stages of my life prior to coming to Spain. If anything, there was quite an air of fear about generally, both amongst the female and male staffs. Most of them were very nice to us, but were they were all quite timid too. They were afraid to do anything that the school authorities wouldn't approve of, even such ordinary human things as going for a drink in the village once a week. And at the same time, everybody tried so hard to be so nice that at times you got the feeling that it was all false, that they all wore masks, even to themselves. They were too perfect. They tried too hard to be too perfect. Everything and everyone was shipshape in a way. All the perfection extended to dress too. None of the female teachers ever wore trousers or jeans, even after work. It just wasn't done. But both Veronica and I used to change into jeans after work. Another black mark against us. Sometimes you longed for someone to turn up for supper in some old clothes and just be human for a change. But they never did. It was intensely irritating after a while.

When we were there about two months, we were called to the principle's office in the boys' school one Friday afternoon after lunch. Immediately we sensed that something was up. But we were quite unprepared for what followed. Carmen translated the principle's speech for us. We were fired. They would pay us one weeks' salary in lieu of notice and we were to leave immediately. We were flabbergasted. There had been no warning that anything like this was on the cards. Worse, we had been flown there on a one-way ticket and had no way of getting home. Besides it was now late autumn and we knew that if there were no jobs to be had last summer, there certainly wouldn't be any at that time of year so it would be the dole queue for both of us. But the one thing we were sure of was that we had both signed a contract which stipulated one month's notice. So we said that they should give us a month's salary in lieu in keeping with the terms of the contract. A long argument ensued. It was clear that both the principle and the Gnasher were furious with us. They went off to consider what we had said, leaving us with Carmen. It was then that she told us that she was a member of Opus Dei and that many of the other teachers were also. When we asked her to explain what that meant, she opened her handbag and took from it a small book called *El Camino* and said that members of Opus Dei lived by that. It was to do with being a good Catholic and a good Christian. For her that meant being a good wife and mother and doing her job well. But as neither Veronica nor I could read or speak much Spanish we couldn't make any judgement about the contents of the book. Carmen also told us that the school was not directly an Opus Dei school. If it was, she said, it would be much stricter. It was just that many of the teachers who worked there were members of Opus Dei. It seemed to us that it didn't make much difference that the school wasn't officially an Opus Dei school if most of the teachers were members of it. But Carmen insisted that there was a big difference; it was just that we didn't see it, as indeed, we didn't. Eventually the principle and the Gnasher returned. They conceded our point concerning the one month's salary and within a short time, we were each handed our pay for the previous month plus a month in lieu, in cash. It made quite a pile of money. Even so we were both in a state of shock. Neither of us had ever got the sack from anywhere before and even though we wanted to leave the school, we didn't want to leave it that way. Besides the shock, I also felt a deep sense of shame as I think Veronica also did. You could sense it between us. It seemed such a shameful thing to be fired. But before we could even discuss how we were going to leave, the Gnasher escorted us out the front door of the boys' school where all the pupils were assembled. In front of the entire assembly he made a speech which we

gathered was a 'thank you' speech to both of us and good
wishes on our journey back to Irlanda. We couldn't believe
our ears. The insincerity of that speech and the false, gnash-
ing smile on his face as he shook hands with us added to the
theatricality of the occasion. He led the students in applause
for us, then sent them back to their afternoon classes, and sent
us off to pack our bags. When classes finished we were given
a lift on the school bus to San Sebastian and that was the last
we saw of Colegio Izarra.

We found bed and breakfast accomodation and over the next
few days decided that we would stay in Spain for the year if
we could find jobs. It was a bank holiday week-end when we
arrived in San Sebastian and we were rather worried to be
carrying so much cash with us. We decided to keep the
money on our persons until it could be deposited in a bank, in
case it would be stolen from our luggage. But as we each had
quite a large pile of pesetas in notes it was difficult to decide
where and how to keep the money safely. Eventually we
stuffed the bulk of it into our socks and limped around San
Sebastian that weekend, since the money made it difficult to
walk normally. Limping along the seafront of the beautiful
beach there one day, we had a rather a surreal encounter. We
saw this fellow coming towards us, guitar slung over his
shoulder, limping, as we were. We started to laugh, because
we guessed that he had money in his socks too. We got talking and it turned out that he was a busker from Dublin. We
had dinner together, the three of us, that evening and in fact,
he had money concealed in his socks. But that was about the
only amusing thing that happened there. It was quite a wor-
rying time. After the bank holiday weekend was over, we
contacted language schools in San Sebastian and in all the
neighbouring towns and eventually struck lucky, landing
jobs in a language school in Vitoria, ironically the nearest
town to the school that had fired us.

We got a flat without too much trouble in Vitoria and stayed there that year teaching English. I did not enjoy that time at all. There were interesting times certainly, because it was the centre of the Basque region and hardly a week went by without a protest march of one kind or another taking place. I took part in one of them, more for some way to pass an evening than for any ideological reason. But because Finland had been such a wonderful experience, nothing afterwards could measure up to it. Besides I missed the friends I made there very much and though we corresponded regularly, life was not as warm as it had been when we were all together in Helsinki. We got to know people through work of course, but as far as I was concerned, they weren't friends in the true sense but more acquaintances, because we had nothing very much in common except that we did the same job and socialised together in the bars most evenings. However, it was fun at first. When we settled in, we felt like we had escaped from prison which we had in a way, and went out on the town most nights. We found the Spanish and Basque custom of having one drink in a bar before moving on to the next one great fun. Our evenings out became like one great big pub-crawl. Unlike the Finns and the Swiss we discovered that the Basques and the Spanish were very extrovert and sometimes we seemed to collect people as we went from bar to bar, ending the evening as a huge crowd going gaily from one to the other. Some of our crowd were into smoking hash which I disliked very much; I had tried it once when I was a student in Dublin and found it disgusting. I remember ending one particular evening in a night-club where we sat around in a circle with joints being passed until the small hours of the morning. I always let it by-pass me and that irritated some of the others. That was the lowest point of that year in Vitoria as far as I was concerned. It seemed to be so futile, sitting there, with the joints circulating and people talking more and more rubbish as they got stoned.

More and more, I felt that this was an aimless kind of way to spend my life. After we left Colegio Izarra I didn't care if I never saw the inside of a church again. I had enough of religion. But as time went on the feeling of aimlessness gave way to a kind of restlessness, and I found as I had in Helsinki, that I needed God in my life; I needed someone to turn to, someone who would understand every twist and turn I took without my having to explain it. What was more, I found that I needed to turn to him not only as an individual but as part of a community. So I went to the local church on Sundays. It was such a contrast to Colegio Izarra. There was a folk group there and everyone joined in the songs in a very lively Spanish sort of way. Going there quelled my sense of restlessness, but not the ever-growing conviction that my life there was aimless somehow.

In the spring Veronica decided that she wanted to stay on in Vitoria the following year and wanted to make arrangements to rent some place to live for the long term. By then I knew that I definitely wanted to go. So we went our separate ways and eventually I returned to Ireland. Through a friend I got a job as a substitute teacher in Cork for a couple of months, then taught English to foreign students for a while. By this time I had made up my mind to do the doctorate in philosophy, no matter what. So I returned to Dublin the following autumn, determined to do the doctorate. It was the research for that which took me through what I later came to realise were documents of the experience of transcendence; the kind of sources which I returned to in an attempt to answer Ginnie's third question.

CHAPTER 10

Reason and revelation

My doctoral research was based on the work of the twentieth century philosopher and political scientist Eric Voegelin, whose writings focused on the problem of order in history. It was he who alerted me to the sequence of similar insights into human nature which were achieved globally during the remarkable period between 800-300 BC which Henri Bergson described as the period of 'the opening of the soul.' During that time there was an awakening of the consciousness of human beings as to their own nature in different cultures and civilisations. It occurred simultaneously in Hellas, in the time of the philosophers; in Israel, in the age of the prophets; in China, in the age of Confucius and Lao Tse; in India, in the age of the Upanishads and the Buddha; and in Persia, in the age of Zarathustra. The feature of that period which I found to be most intriguing was the fact that notwithstanding the plurality of different beliefs and their corresponding modes of symbolic expression, there was a remarkable sameness of human experience underlying them, particularly the experience of the individual in search of the ground of reality. Voegelin's approach in particular interested me because he noted that while comparative studies of societies focused on the phenomenon of 'equivalent' cults, ceremonies, rites and myths, there was no such adequate language for dealing with the quest of the individual for meaning concerning his or her origin and end. However in so looking for such a language of 'equivalences', one must be aware that the sameness which justifies it does not lie in the symbols themselves, but rather in the experiences which have engendered them. The reason for that was simply that an exploration of the past from any perspective whatsoever reveals that what is permanent in the history of mankind is not the symbols but man himself in search of his humanity and its order. So anyone who embarks on the search for the ground of reality does not begin in a *terra incognita*, but rather moves among symbols concerning the truth of existence which represent the experience of his or her predecessors. Thus the study of symbols, will become, if fully developed, a language enabling one to relate to other beliefs and their symbolic expression on account of the experiential equivalence underlying all of them, without making a claim to absolute superiority or supremacy for one's own. From the beginning this approach struck me as a way out of the impasse wrought by conflicting claims to truth which were, and are, a constant feature of human life, particularly in the area of religious belief and practice.

So I propose to answer Ginnie's third question, 'Is it still a case of "outside the Roman Catholic Church there is no salvation?"' by drawing on the philosophical tradition guided by the insights and analysis of Eric Voegelin. It might seem a peculiar way to deal with a question that seems at face value to be a purely theological one. But that is where I have found most clarity on the subject of what human beings are and how they relate to a divine source of reality who is conventionally named God. Besides, the church's own treatment of this question is, to my mind, woefully inadequate.

The Catechism of the Catholic Church attempts to deal with the problems embedded in the affirmation 'Outside the church there is no salvation' by quoting from the dogmatic constitution on the church, *Lumen Gentium*, which was issued by the Second Vatican Council: 'Basing itself on scripture and tradition, (the second Vatican council) teaches that the church, a pilgrim now on earth, is necessary for salvation: the one Christ is mediator and the way of salvation; he is present to us in his body which is the church. He himself explicitly asserted the necessity of faith and baptism, and thereby affirmed at the same time the necessity of the church which men enter through baptism as through a door. Hence they could not be saved who, knowing that the Catholic Church was founded as necessary by God through Christ, would refuse either to enter it, or to remain in it.' Moreover the *Catechism* asserts that re-formulated positively, this simply means that all salvation comes from Christ the head through the church which is his body; it is not aimed at those who, through no fault of their own, do not know Christ and his church. To underline this point it restates the position of *Lumen Gentium* concerning all who seek God with a sincere heart: 'those too may achieve eternal salvation.' So far as the institutional church is concerned, that includes presumably people like Canon Kennerley and the Chinese student I met in Finland. I wonder how comforting it is to people who are not Roman Catholics to know that the Roman Catholic Church considers that they *may* be saved?

I consider the *Catechism's* explanation of the formula 'outside the church there is no salvation' to be inadequate for two reasons. Firstly, because underlying the specific formula itself there is a claim to truth concerning the relationship between human beings and God by the Roman Catholic Church which relegates insights by all other denominations to the status of falsehood. For notwithstanding the fact that *Lumen Gentium* adds qualifications to include catechumens, other Christian denominations, and others who both believe in and seek a divine Creator, and states that these are also included in the plan of salvation, there is no getting around the absolute nature of the Roman Catholic claim to be the sole means of salvation. The *Catechism* completely evades the issues inherent in that claim.

And secondly, because it does not explain how Christ can be both the head of the Roman Catholic Church, outside of which there is no salvation, and the head of all mankind, or as

the *Catechism* puts it, 'Christ is Lord of the cosmos and of history'. This problem has been beautifully expressed by Eric
Voegelin: 'For it is the Christ of the Gospel of John who says
of himself: "Before Abraham was, I am' (8:58); and it is
Thomas Aquinas who considers the Christ to be the head of
the *corpus mysticum* that embraces, not only Christians, but all
mankind from the creation of the world to its end. In practice
this means that one has to recognise, and make intelligible,
the presence of Christ in a Babylonian hymn, or a Taoist spec-
ulation, or a Platonic dialogue, just as much as in a gospel.'

It seems to me that the church cannot deal with the problem
of explaining how Christ is the head of all mankind and not
just Christians because all its attempts at articulating the revelation of God in the person of Jesus Christ rely on the false
dichotomy between natural reason and supernatural revelation. Such a distinction is empirically unsustainable since the
history of the world up to the present time is littered with
documentary evidence of revelatory experiences. Therefore,
imposing a framework on those experiences which relies on a
medieval theological distinction such as 'natural reason' and
'supernatural revelation' makes no sense at all from the
scholarly perspective. It may very well be that it can be maintained in an exclusively theological context where it has to do
with the problems of an ecclesiastical organisation such as the
Roman Catholic Church. However, to my mind, the church's
rigid adherence to an excessively narrow interpretation of the
distinction between natural reason and supernatural revelation is the cause of much of its problems at the present time,
particularly relating to the role of women. For such a narrow
interpretation of the distinction between reason and revelation underlies the church's self-description and self-defini-
tion of its structures and organisation as male, celibate and
hierarchical. It does not however use such explicit terms as
those I have used. Instead the *Catechism* teaches that the
church was instituted according to the divine plan of God the

Father by Jesus Christ and the Holy Spirit; that it was given the mission of proclaiming that Jesus is the Christ who will save the world from itself; that it was endowed 'with a structure that will remain until the Kingdom is fully achieved' by Jesus Christ's choice of twelve male apostles with Peter as their head; and that these men and their male successors were entrusted with the task of choosing the writings which would form the canon of Scripture, interpreting it, and devising forms of faith-life which they deemed appropriate which would be regarded as a sacred tradition. Thus, the church summarises its own description of itself in the *Catechism* as follows: 'The task of interpreting the Word of God authentically has been entrusted solely to the Magisterium of the Church, that is, to the Pope and the bishops in communion with him.'

A more critical issue however, is that the church is unable to explain how Christ is the head of all mankind and not just Christians because all its attempts rely on the false dichotomy between natural reason and supernatural revelation. For example, the *Catechism of the Catholic Church* states: 'By natural reason man can know God with certainty, on the basis of his works. But there is another order of knowledge, which man cannot possibly arrive at by his own powers: the order of divine Revelation.' And according to the church the divine plan of Revelation involves a specific divine pedagogy, that is, 'God communicates himself to man gradually. He prepares him to welcome by stages the supernatural Revelation that is to culminate in the person and mission of the Incarnate Word, Jesus Christ.' And it continues: 'The Word of God, which is the power of God for salvation to everyone who has faith, is set forth and displays its power in a most wonderful way in the writings of the New Testament which hand on the ultimate truth of God's Revelation.'

The difficulty I have with that way of looking at things is that implicit in the statement that the New Testament is 'the *ulti-*

mate truth of God's Revelation', is the judgement that all other forms of the experience of divine presence are inferior in some way. However to hold that God *only* reveals himself imperfectly and provisionally in the Old Testament and fully and completely in the New Testament; and that every other culture and tradition which comes to a knowledge of the divine does so through the inferior medium of natural reason, is impermissible from the scholarly perspective. For when one looks at the history of the world one can find testimonies of the experience of transcendence at all times and in all cultures. Such testimonies include ancient constructions which symbolised man's relation with the divine exemplified superbly by Newgrange; cave paintings from ancient civilisations; the observance of sacred days and festivals in various cultures; and the written documents of revelatory experiences such as those of the period 800-300 BC exemplified in Greece by the work of the poets, tragedians and philosophers; in China by the *Analects* of Confucius and the *Tao* of Lao-tze; in India by the *Upanishads*; and in Persia by the *Avestas*. These contribute to the formidable body of evidence that there is such a thing as a revelatory experience which transcends the boundaries of culture and tradition. Moreover, that the body of evidence exists also testifies to the *how* of such experiences of transcendence in that it points to human nature as its source.

St Paul was clearly aware of the different ways God revealed himself to human beings. In the Acts of the Apostles which record the speech he gave at the Council of the Areopagus in Athens he addresses the people beginning, 'Athenians, I see how extremely religious you are in every way. For as I went through the city and looked carefully at the objects of your worship, I found among them an altar with the inscription, "To an Unknown God." What therefore you worship as unknown, this I proclaim to you ... For "in him we live and move and have our being"; as even some of your own poets recognised that revelation was a process in history in which the Unknown God ultimately becomes the God known through his presence in Christ. However he does not use sources from traditions other than his own to illustrate how this is so; perhaps because he himself is sufficiently persuaded from the evidence within the Jewish tradition. As he puts it in the letter to the Hebrews: 'At various times in the past and in various different ways, God spoke to our ancestors through the prophets; but in our own time, the last days, he has spoken to us through his Son, the Son that he has appointed to inherit everything and through whom he made everything there is.'

Nevertheless the evidence from other traditions serves to illustrate further the revelation of the Unknown God in history. For example in the Egypt of the thirteenth century BC. there can be discerned a strong movement towards an understanding of the hidden divinity beyond the cosmological gods of the local culture. This is explicitly recorded in the *Amon Hymns* of Dynasty XIX which tell of the first God 'who came into being at the beginning, so that his mysterious nature is unknown'. He hides himself behind the form of the local known gods, thus remaining hidden and invisible, and even his name is unknown. However the Unknown God is not a new god but rather the divine reality experienced as present also in the known gods. Thus behind the known Egyptian deities there is the sense of the Unknown God from whom they derive their divine reality; and though those cosmological gods are derivative, they are not nevertheless false, since they participate in the divine reality of the Unknown God. In this context it is interesting to note that several hundred years later in Greece there is a record of an equivalent insight to that of the *Amon Hymns* by Aristotle in the *Metaphysics* where he stated that 'the Prime Mover is a beginning absolutely.' It is clear that the authors of both the *Amon Hymns* and the *Metaphysics* recognised the notion of 'in the beginning' as the true criterion of divine reality.

Of particular interest, however, when looking at the expressions of experience of human beings that can be discerned in the early history of philosophy, is the recognition of different modes of expressing the same truth. Aristotle was the first to record this in his *Metaphysics*. He noted that the ancient poets such as Homer and Hesiod considered the gods and goddesses to be the ground of things and among their pantheon of deities was one named *Okeonos*, the god of the ocean whom Homer, in the *Iliad*, described as 'the primal source of all that lives'. However in his historical survey of the Ionian philosophers, Aristotle noted that Thales the Milesian is generally credited with being the first thinker to raise the question of the nature and origin of everything that exists and hence could be regarded as the founder of philosophy. But he maintained that the insight of Thales, that the origin of all things was water, was actually the same as that of Homer; the difference between them being the fact that they expressed their insights in different symbols. Thus, the mythological symbol *Okeonos* is actually the equivalent of the philosophical symbol 'water'; in that though the symbols themselves differ, the experience underlying them, that is the sense that reality is constituted by water, is the same. But what is even more interesting according to Aristotle, is the sense of both the poet and the philosopher that the first substance out of which all things come is divine and he refers to this sense that 'the divine encloses the whole of nature' to be 'an inspired utterance'. Furthermore because the source of origin of both the myth-makers and the philosopher's inquiry was the experience of wonder, Aristotle concluded that 'the lover of myths is in a sense a lover of wisdom'. In other words, the *philomythos* is in a sense a *philosophos* on account of the sameness of experience underlying their different symbols. So as far as Aristotle was concerned, a myth such as those created by Homer was not lie or falsehood, but rather a truth expressed in a different mode. And as if to emphasise his commitment to the truths of myth as well as philosophy,

Aristotle stated in a letter in his old age: 'The more I am by myself and alone, the more I have come to love myths.' Thus when one looks at the expressions of the experience of searching for the ground of reality in the early history of philosophy, what is striking, besides the variety of symbols that are to be found, is the generous recognition and tolerance extended to rival symbolisations of the same truth with Aristotle being the first person who recorded this sense of pluralism in expressing truth.

But though Aristotle was the first to record such pluralism, there is no doubt that his immediate predecessor Plato was also of a pluralist cast of mind when it came to expressing insights into the nature of reality as a whole since there is a very real sense of an unknown and unknowable divinity behind Plato's variety of symbols for the ground of being. For example in a famous passage in the *Republic* known as 'the story of the ascent from the cave' Plato analyses very carefully the situation of the individual who is thrown into a reality of which he knows neither origin or end, nor indeed, how he is to live within it. He is depicted as sometimes experiencing a sense of wonder at the way his reality is, and from that initial sense of wondering, is impelled to seek answers. That seeking and searching is allied to questioning, sometimes joyfully and willingly. However, at other times there is the sense of feeling moved to ask questions about the nature of reality by some unknown force; and at other times again, there is a sense of feeling drawn into the search by something outside and beyond oneself. In that way Plato suggests that the individual is impelled to turn around from the darkness of ignorance to the light of knowledge, and recognise that a source which he names as the *Agathon* or 'the Beyond' is the source of everything. However the *Agathon* is essentially unknown so that nothing can really be said about it; but the vision itself forms the individual through an experience of transcendence. Thus the *Agathon* symbolises the essence of the Unknown

God which the Egyptian Amon Hymns and the Aristotelian Prime Mover also attempted to express. Moreover in his analysis of the situation of an individual who is puzzled about reality as a whole, Plato is meticulous in his attention to the stages of that experience. His carefully chosen verbs indicate that these stages include those of *wondering, seeking, searching, questioning, feeling moved and feeling drawn by some unknown force, and being impelled to turn around* to see the origin and source of everything, insofar as it is capable of being perceived by human beings. Furthermore in order to indicate that our knowledge of that source can only be a partial knowledge, Plato created many other symbols to depict his insight into what it is. Among these are 'the Player of the Puppets' which occurs in Plato's *Laws*.

This is a particularly interesting symbol because, it illustrates the common ground between classic philosophy and the gospels. In each of them there is the same sense of the individual being pulled and drawn by some force or presence outside himself; the same sense of participating in a reality characterised by the divine-human relationship; and the same experience of divine reality as the centre of action in the movement from question to answer. For that reason, it provides an interesting challenge to the dictum 'Outside the church there is no salvation.'

In attempting to answer the question 'How should one live?' Plato presents the situation of the human being as that of an individual living in a world of attractions and counter-attractions. The various options or existential states open to him or her are symbolised by cords made of metals of various kinds, all of which pull the individual in different directions and all of which are opposed to each other. All of the metals are hard and iron-like, with one exception. That is the golden cord which is soft and pliable and the pull from it to the individual is gentle and without violence. Moreover in order to prevail in existence, it needs the support and co-operation of the individual who, in choosing it, must counter-pull against the pull of the cords of base metal. The golden cord represents reason, which is the most divine part of the individual and, in the conflict between it and the various metal cords, the individual learns that its duty is to live according to reason. In this way Plato symbolises the individual as a being who is free to choose how to live. Behind the symbol lies the field of existence with attractions and counter-attractions. Plato pinpoints the individual's rejection of the pull of the golden cord of reason as the source of confusion and meaninglessness and alienation. Thus implicit in Plato's symbol of the 'Player of the Puppets' is the self-condemnation of the individual to a life without meaning; for anyone who complains about the nature of existence is pointing to his or her own rejection of the 'Player' who pulls the golden cord.

This experience of the Unknown God as one who gently tugs people towards himself has also been symbolised by St John in the fourth gospel as 'the Father who draws all people to himself'. The symbolism of 'drawing' is unique to St John and does not occur elsewhere in the New Testament. By using it St John actually symbolises the pull of the golden cord as Plato did; though for St John, the pull of the golden cord occurred as an historical event in the person Jesus Christ. However though Jesus speaks of drawing all people to himself, the drawing power which he exerts is both identified with, and has its origin in, the pull of the Unknown God, whom St John symbolises as 'the Father'. In the fourth gospel, Jesus explicitly uses this term: 'No one can come to me unless drawn by the Father who sent me.'

Plato's 'Player of the Puppets' and St John's 'Father who draws all people to himself' are both symbolisations of the Unknown God who reveals himself in time. For Plato, the *presence* of the Unknown God is experienced and symbolised in a variety of ways through his dialogues. St John on the other hand relied on the literary form of letting a narrative of events be followed by an exposition of their meaning through the response of Jesus. However the literary form is itself the testament of St John's *personal experience* of being drawn by Christ who mediates the drawing power of God the Father. As such, a gospel is not a mere record of information; it is rather a record of the revelation of God in history. Such a revelation is not given through any information spoken by Jesus since it demands the individual's *response* to the full presence of the Unknown God in him.

That the Unknown God reveals himself in time and space is attested by the trail of symbols in history. Moreover the different symbolisations of the insight that the Unknown God is revealing himself in history throws into relief the process of revelation itself. For what is revealed in all cultures through a variety of symbols is the presence of divine reality in human consciousness in different ways. This in turn illuminates what it is to be a human being. Various attempts have been made by philosophers in all ages to come up with a definition of what it means to be human, going back to Aristotle who characterised man as the *zoon noetikon*, that is, 'the living being who possesses reason'. Moreover it was through the faculty and activity of nous or reason that the divine presence revealed itself to human beings. Through the Latin translation of *zoon noetikon* as *animal rationale*, man was defined as the 'rational animal' and this phrase subsequently became a popular definition of what it was to be a human being. But the twentieth century philosopher Ernst Cassirer noted that 'reason' and 'rationality' are very inadequate terms with which to comprehend the forms of human beings' cultural life in all their richness and variety. So Cassirer proposed that instead of defining human beings as *animal rationale*, we should define them as *animal symbolicum* because in doing so, we can designate the specific difference of human life more precisely. However, in another attempt to pinpoint more accurately what it meant to be human, Eric Voegelin shifted the focus from the emphasis on the physical, corporeal being who has so much in common with other organisms to its most distinctive feature, that is, its ability to express its inner life. It is this approach to what human beings are that I find most helpful as it is one that sets out most explicitly how we are aware of, and relate to God.

One particularly striking image which Voegelin uses to explain that relationship is drawn from the theatre. Human beings are not spectators of reality. They are more like actors, playing their part in the drama of being, and through the very fact of their existence, committed to playing it without knowing what it is. Both their own specific roles, and the play as a whole is unknown. So for the individual, there is a sense of participating in existence without knowledge of how it is going to work out. This lack of knowledge is ignorance in the true sense of the word. It can be, and for a great many people very often is, profoundly disturbing. For there is no vantage point outside existence from which its meaning can be viewed and a course of action charted; nor is there an island somewhere where one can permanently withdraw from it. The life of the individual must be lived out in the uncertainty of life's meaning, and one can approach it with any one of a number of attitudes ranging from adventure to angst. However, the individual who is sensitive to his or her own experience realises that the situation is neither one of complete ignorance nor complete darkness. He or she has an in-built light so to speak, in that human beings are illuminated by consciousness. And it is that consciousness, if used, that enables the individual to discern that he or she is not alone in an alien land but rather, moving among symbols concerning the truth of existence which represent the experiences of his or her predecessors. Moreover, the concern of the individual about the meaning of life does not have to remain pent up in the tortures of anxiety, but can vent itself in the creation of symbols which attempt to make his or her experience of reality intelligible. So with that in mind Voegelin came up with the description of human beings as 'the creator of symbols'. However given the global phenomenon of the experience of searching for meaning in existence and its expression in different ways, he noted that there are four typical features to be discerned in the process of symbolisation throughout the world.

Firstly, there is the sense of the experience of *participation* in being. That, is to say, whatever human beings may be, they know themselves to be a *part* of a greater reality. Secondly, there is the preoccupation with the lasting and the passing of the things that exist. One person lasts while others pass away and eventually she passes away while others last on. All human beings are outlasted by the society of which they are members, and eventually the societies pass while the world lasts. Because of this there is the sense that the world itself is outlasted by the gods; perhaps it was even created by them. In this way reality manifests the structure of a hierarchy of existence, ranging from the ephemeral lowliness of plants and animals and human beings to the everlastingness of the gods. This *experience* of the hierarchy of existence provides an important piece of knowledge which can, and does, become a force in ordering the lives of human beings. That is, when we discover that we are thrown in and out of existence without knowing why or how, we learn to attune ourselves to what is lasting, of which we are but a part. In this way Voegelin suggests, we learn the difference between 'existing' and 'being': 'In existing, we experience mortality; in being we experience what can be symbolised by the negative metaphor of immortality.' A third feature in the expression of the experience of participation in a reality which is characterised by durability and transiency is the attempt at making the essentially unknowable order of being intelligible as far as possible through the creation of symbols which interpret the unknown by analogy with the known. And finally, there is the awareness on the part of the creator of symbols of the analogical character of the symbols he or she has created.

A glance at the range of symbolic forms in all cultures reveals the immense richness and complexity of their creators: language, myth, art, music, ritual, philosophy, and so on. Furthermore these reveal a *tendency* in human beings to go beyond themselves and reach towards the ground of existence itself . This 'ground' is expressed in a variety of ways in different cultures at all times in history; for example, linguistically as 'Amon' or 'the divine' or 'the First Mover' or 'God' or 'Allah'; artistically, in the paintings and sculptures of gods in all cultures and societies; and musically in for example the passion of Handel's *Messiah* or Haydn's *Te Deum*. That there is such a tendency in human nature to transcend itself is undeniable, since the documentary evidence is there in the trail of symbols throughout the course of history.

The diversity of symbols in various cultures indicates that a basic human experience and insight is that the Unknown God is the origin and end of everything. Moreover for reasons which are known only to the divine presence itself, the manifestations of divinity range through the hierarchy of being from the inorganic, to the vegetative, to the animal, to the human – in the person of Jesus Christ. Thus the Unknown God becomes the known God through his presence in Christ – to those whose consciousness is attuned to it in the manner described by St Paul in Colossians: 'In him the whole fullness of divine reality dwells bodily.' For the disciples and those contemporaries of Christ who accepted his divinity, there must have been something extraordinarily impressive about him such that his entire being appeared to be fully permeated by the divine presence. However Christ himself cautioned about insisting on bodily proofs of divinity in his response to Thomas: 'You believe because you can see me. Happy are those who have not seen and yet believe.'

The *Amon Hymns* of ancient Egypt and the writings of the ancient Greek philosophers along with many other symbols from all cultures are documentary evidence of the experience of transcendence. There is no doubt that the authors of such documents were anything but aware that they were having a revelation of a kind when they were drawn into a conscious awareness of the reality of the Unknown God – before he made himself known in the person of Jesus Christ. But those revelations of his divinity are not any the less real for being manifest in different ways. Such documents of the experience of transcendence are not logical proofs by any means, nor do they pretend to be. But as documents of the experience of the divine presence, they invite the reader to look in the direction they indicate. One cannot have more.

Nevertheless what I find missing from the Roman Catholic Church's account of the reality of human life and of how human beings relate to the divine presence is the sense of how the experience of God can be symbolised in different ways, and be none the less inferior for all that. Somewhere along the way in the formulation of its doctrine the church has allowed doctrinal formulations to separate from the experience of the mystery on which it was founded. In other words, the mystery of the revelatory process of the Unknown God becoming known in various ways as well as in the person of Jesus of Galilee, has become fossilised into the God of the Creed. The development of doctrine and dogma is not problematic in itself, since it is a socially and culturally necessary protection of insights which were gained experientially, against false propositions. As such it is secondary to the truth of experience. However, when doctrinal formulations are endowed with autonomy and authority such that they become separated from the truth of experience, it has the unfortunate consequence of allowing an attitude of 'If you are not with us, you are against us' to flourish; unfortunate, because the insistence is on adherence to the letter of the doctrinal formulation, rather than the spirit of the gospel, which it was developed to protect. So because I find the body of evidence concerning the revelation of the God to human beings at all times and in all cultures so persuasive, I cannot accept that 'outside the Roman Catholic Church there is no salvation.' No doubt there are those who will say that I am not a real Roman Catholic at all because of that, but so be it. I just hope Ginnie will understand.

The diversity of views within the Roman Catholic Church should be an indication of how healthy it is, given the level of commitment to the gospel they manifest, as well as the passion with which they are very often articulated. However, very often any discussion of what the gospel has to offer the present age and the next millennium degenerates into a kind of ecclesiastical dog-fighting where judgements such as 'fundamentalist' and 'liberal' are thrown about, after which there is a retreat to the trenches on both sides. And with all of it, the human community is the real loser, in both the short and long term because such polarisation inevitably breeds suspicion and mistrust, which are the very antitheses of the new commandment 'Love one another.'

CHAPTER 11

Religious groups

When I began my attempt to answer Virginia Kennerley's three questions I found that when I tried to find reasons for being a Christian and a Roman Catholic, I could not think of any offhand, but that I could think of one very good reason for not being a Christian or not wanting to be one, ever. That reason had to do with my Grandmother's suicide on Christmas Day. But for all the horror and resentment that flowed from that death I found, as the years went by, that there was something stronger than all of that. That 'something', no matter where I went, was what I can only describe as 'a sense of the sacred' permeating through the whole known world as well as my own personal reality. It is probably a very inadequate phrase but it articulates my experience as clearly as it is possible to do in words. But in the aftermath of Grandmother's lonely death it drove me demented and my response to it was to clam my heart tightly shut, like an oyster, to lock it out of my life. However in my bleakest moments that sense of the sacred re-appeared as the only hope there was and I gratefully responded to it and in so doing, found the strength to carry on. But when I was up and running, the old sores festered and the resentment took over and the cycle began again, with me locking God out of my heart, telling him to get out of my life; to leave me alone because he wasn't wanted; because I didn't want him; because I hated him for not lifting a finger to help Grandmother as she lay dying on the dark on Christmas night or Kitty either when she couldn't live without Grandmother. Later on, when I began my research for the doctorate I discovered that besides the trail of symbols that testified to the insights of people everywhere that the ground of existence was divine, there was also extant a trail of symbols that testified to the experience of closure to the divine ground, with its accompanying existential disorder. So an attitude of closure to the sacred such as mine was by no means a unique phenomenon but was in fact as well documented as was the experience of the sacred, in all cultures at all times.

Two thinkers struck me as capturing this experience particularly vividly through the language-symbols they created: Plato and St Thomas Aquinas. In his dialogues Plato made a distinction between 'reason' *(nous)* and 'unreason' *(anoia)* which for the most part has been lost sight of in academic philosophy. Being 'reasonable' means being intellectually open so that questions concerning the ground of being may be raised, even though they may point towards a divine ground as the answer; whereas being 'unreasonable' means being intellectually closed to such questions. St Thomas Aquinas had a similar insight as Plato's, though he developed it further by characterising the different ways and degrees of closure as a turning away from the divine ground *(aversio a Deo)*; and a turning away combined with negating the divine presence and building an interpretation of reality on the repudiation of God *(conversio ad creaturam)*.

For years after Grandmother's death, I experienced long periods of intellectual closure to any questions which might lead to affirm the ground of reality as divine. It was an attitude of being which was quite distinct from clinical depression but one which fuelled it somehow. But none of the psychiatrists who treated me when I was young displayed any awareness of the reality of experiences and attitudes rooted in the human spirit, and what role they played in the maintenance of mental health. However as I grew older and eventually learned the difference between the two, I knew that I was freely responsible for not only my mental well-being but also my intellectual and spiritual well-being. The intellectual side of things was no problem because of my immersion in philosophy and academic life. Neither was the mental, because now that I knew what breakdown and depression were, I learned coping mechanisms for dealing with the black cloud whenever it struck again. But the spiritual side of things was different. I just could not sustain a spiritual life for very long. Whenever I went back to Mass I found it satisfying for a few months or so, and then stopped going and locked God out of my life once more. So any spiritual dimension there was in my life was a very sporadic one, sometimes being eclipsed for years on end.

That changed when, after browsing in Parson's Bookshop one Saturday afternoon, I came across a book called *The Way* by Josemaria Escriva. I recognised the name instantly as the author of the little book *El Camino* which the English teacher in Colegio Izarra had shown us, the book which was used by members of Opus Dei. I leafed through it out of sheer curiosity and was immediately struck by its quite extraordinary passion and sincerity and idealism. So I bought it and spent that evening reading it, going over and over again some of the reflections which touched me particularly. I couldn't understand how Opus Dei had the extraordinary bad name it had in the village of Izarra or why no-one at the school had explained to us that this was what it was about. It struck me as an uniquely practical way of living the gospels and I spent the next few weeks reading and re-reading it, renewing my determination to try, once again, to live according to the gospels with its help. Eventually curiosity got the better of me and I wrote to the Opus Dei Information Office, which was listed in the telephone directory, asking for information about the organisation. However because of what I had heard about the organisation when I was in Spain, I half expected to receive no reply at all, being sure that my name was listed in some big black book somewhere as 'the enemy'. But I did receive a reply, a very courteous prompt reply at that, with some information leaflets; and it was suggested that if I wanted any further information, to contact their university residence for female students, Glenard. I thought about it for a while and eventually decided to make contact, thinking that I might as well find out at first hand what it was all about. So I did and that was the beginning of my association with Opus Dei.

During my first meeting with the director of Glenard, I told her about my time in Spain and what I knew of Opus Dei from there. She was quite puzzled and assured me that Colegio Izarra was not run directly by the organisation at all; it must be an independently owned school which employed some people who were Opus Dei members. At that stage it didn't matter to me one way or the other because from the very beginning I liked what I saw in Glenard. Everyone I met was very friendly, and I began to go along to weekly recollections there. These were a sort of *lectio divina*, which lasted about half an hour, with one of the Opus Dei clergy taking a passage from Scripture and giving a talk about it. I found those sessions very helpful and looked forward to going to them and it was through them that I began to see what Opus Dei taught: that it was necessary to devise a plan of life in order to develop one's spiritual life, in the same way that one has to devise a programme of training if one is to get physically fit. Afterwards I discovered that the particular format used in the university residence was geared specifically for students who were just beginning to explore what faith was all about. Otherwise the format was called a circle, and this was actually an informal gathering of a few people in one of the members' homes for prayer. The circle was always led by one of the group; there was no priest present. But there was a monthly recollection given by the clergy for the various circles.

The circle I attended was given by a member of Opus Dei, though those of us who attended it were not. We were actually quite a mixed bag in terms of ages and interests, but it was a very friendly group and I really enjoyed meeting them. It was the first time in my life that religion began to make sense to me. The basic spirituality of Opus Dei was that God could be found through one's life and work; that he wasn't the exclusive property of priests and nuns. So in order to live a Christian life it was important to take one's spiritual formation seriously, which meant reading the Scriptures and attending Mass and confession regularly; taking responsibility for one's intellectual and spiritual formation through reading and attendance at circles and recollections, and then putting it into practise in the situation of one's life and work, whatever that happened to be. There was something radically new in the way Opus Dei communicated the gospels which I found very attractive. And besides, through it I got to know many other people, all of whom were attempting to live the spirit of the gospels with the help of the spirituality of Opus Dei, so there was a real sense of friendship and community at the recollections because everyone knew everyone else. It was so different to the cold impersonality of parish life. In the early stages of my acquaintance with the organisation, I thought that eventually I might join it and talked the possibility over with the director of Glenard. Opus Dei seemed to me the perfect support network I needed to help me sustain a spiritual life while immersed in the professional world.

It wasn't all plain sailing though. There were aspects of the spiritual practises of the numerary and associate members of Opus Dei which I found both unhealthy and distasteful. These included the use of what were called a 'cilis' (or maybe it was 'cilium',(I can't remember exactly) and a 'discipline'. The former was a type of chain with little spikes in it which was worn around the thigh for an hour each day; and the latter was a type of whip made from what looked to me like macramé, which was used to flagellate oneself. The idea behind such physical mortifications as they were called was to identify with the physical suffering inflicted on Christ. When I first began to go to recollections in Glenard I read as much as I could about the organisation, both positive and negative, so had come across references to this type of practise. But it was very difficult to get anyone to talk about it. Eventually through much persistence on my part, one of the girls showed me her chain and whip. She was quite matter of fact about it, accepting it as part of her way of loving Christ. It didn't seem so extraordinary, listening to her, but afterwards whenever I thought about it, it brought images of various kinds of sexual perversions to mind and I thought it was distinctly unhealthy. But so long as no-one expected me to do it, that was fine. And in fact, no one did.

What I found a lot more difficult to take, however, was the demand for absolute loyalty to both the founder of Opus Dei and the Pope. They enjoyed such cult status that it seemed to me that the very essence of Jesus Christ and his teaching was eclipsed. No word of criticism was uttered, ever, by the members and they had no concept at all of constructive criticism being good and healthy in an organisation such as Opus Dei or the Roman Catholic Church itself. It was also a very traditional organisation. However the traditional style of liturgy and music didn't bother me because I quite liked it. But there were no Eucharist ministers or lay readers at the Masses in the centres, though at the annual public Mass there were always lay readers. I found this particularly puzzling in an organisation that publicly encouraged lay spirituality; that such encouragement didn't extend to having lay ministers at its own Masses. However what bothered me increasingly as time went on was the virtual obsession with rules and regulations so that in the end it seemed to me that the organisation was more concerned with the letter of the law rather than the spirit of the gospels. So eventually I stopped going to the circles and recollections. There just wasn't the kind of freedom there that I found in the accounts of Christ's life and relationships with people. Rules and regulations are no substitute for the spirit of the gospels. That does not mean however, that others found it as rule-bound as I did. For the most part, it was like any other organisation in that all of human life was there, in terms of occupations, personalities and temperaments. And it was clear to me that the spirituality and organisational structure of Opus Dei suited most of the people I met through the organisation. It was certainly very helpful to me in that it taught me the importance of nurturing the seed of the gospels through daily personal prayer and for that I will always be grateful to it. But, to use a vineyard metaphor, I found that its particular methods of training and pruning the vines did not suit me because I could not grow and flourish within them. However two of my friends are members of the organisation so there has been a learning experience of 'live and let live' on both sides.

However because I had found the ambience of a group very helpful in that it was personal and ensured that you didn't feel alone in your desire to live according to the gospels, I explored other groups too thinking that maybe one or the other might be a kind of safe harbour for me, where I could retreat to when I needed sanctuary and encouragement when life got difficult. But beyond attending a few initial meetings, I didn't bother. *Focolare* struck me as too charismatic by far and I was embarrassed at the emotional displays I witnessed there. *Communion and Liberation* was a very jolly group, but compared with Opus Dei, it was absolutely chaotic. The few meetings I attended usually started two hours late. No-one seemed to mind, but I found myself wishing for a dose of Opus Dei type efficiency in the administration of the organisation. *The Teresian Association* too was very welcoming and helpful, though it has only a handful of members in Ireland. All of them in fact were extremely welcoming and the people I met very friendly. But it struck me that though they all considered themselves to be different to all other lay organisations, they had one thing in common which I found disquieting. That was what I can only describe as the cult of the founder. I understand that one would naturally want to respect and honour the person who initiated a way of helping people to live their Christianity, but I thought that they had all gone a little overboard in doing so; so much so, that when Christ should have been the orienting centre of the organisation, he seemed displaced by the founder, who was almost deified. And I found that quite distasteful.

I discussed the structure and organisation of groups in a general way with one of my Professors and how I just didn't seem to fit in anywhere. That actually bothered me quite a lot at that time. His answer however, blew away any sense of discomfiture or inferiority I felt, as he wryly observed: 'Some people are clubable. Others are not.' I laughed. What a relief to know that I was quite normal after all. I just wasn't clubable. Just as well the church was as large as it was, in every sense of the word. Because whatever its faults, I felt I belonged in it.

CHAPTER 12

A monument and a name

It is extraordinary how it is when you feel most secure that, out of the blue, something comes along and blows your world apart. And even though Virginia's three questions confronted my sense of security and complacency with all the force of three hand grenades recently, they were as nothing to the atom-bomb I experienced when I first visited Jerusalem. That was after I had encountered the various lay organisations within the church and, having seen what they had to offer, I had settled for being a plain ordinary Christian within the Roman Catholic tradition. But I didn't go as a pilgrim to Jerusalem. In fact I went quite by chance, as a philosopher, to a conference on Ethics in Medicine which was held in the Maale Hahamisha Kibbutz Hotel in the countryside outside Jerusalem. Medical ethics fascinated me because it touched very closely and practically on the issue of how we perceive the human being, which is the fundamental problem of philosophical anthropology, my first philosophical love, so to speak. The conference was as interesting as the programme had promised and I was very happy that I had made the effort to attend it. It lasted the best part of a week and there were trips scheduled in the free time to the sights in Jerusalem and elsewhere. I had thought to go on one of them but during a coffee-break, I was chatting with an Israeli doctor who inquired what my plans were during the free periods and when I said that I would go to see the various Christian sites, she asked, 'Have you been to Yad Vashem?' I didn't quite catch the name so said 'Yad what?' And she exclaimed in a horrified tone: 'You don't know what Yad Vashem is! But you must go there! You must go there if you want to understand anything about the Jewish people.' And then she explained that it was a memorial to the victims of the Holocaust. So that afternoon, instead of going on the official conference trip, I took a taxi to Yad Vashem sensing, as I had sensed so often before, that I wasn't just going there, but was being drawn there, as if by an invisible thread.

It was a huge place. I walked up a long tree-lined avenue and wandered at will through the various buildings scattered around the hill-side without the aid of a map or guide-book. The first building I entered happened to be the poignant Children's Memorial. Portraits, in black and white, of some of the children who had died in the concentration camps gazed down at me; beautiful children, of six and seven and eight and nine years old; dark-eyed and dark skinned; blue-eyed and fair-skinned; smiling and solemn; all of them beautiful; all of them innocent; all of them victims of the Nazi murder machine; all of them dead. I broke down in tears as candles glimmered in the darkness and the names of children who perished were gently relayed over the public address system. Afterwards, outside in the sunshine, somebody's grandfather sat on a bench, breathing heavily, staring dry-eyed and horror stricken into the clear, blue sky. I too found a quiet place to be alone and wept, for the crushed innocents whose memories were so beautifully preserved inside.

It was to be an afternoon of weeping and grieving. For who could not weep at the endless catalogue of photographs of Nazi horror; at the mass grave in Bergen-Belsen; at the sight of the selection platform at Auschwitz; at the sight of Jewish women stripped naked and huddled together before German officers, before being shot and dumped into the open grave at their feet; at the sight of Jews who had tried to escape the camps gruesomely impaled on the barbed wire; at the sight of the corpses, the bones, the gas-chambers, the ovens, the bars of soap made from Jewish flesh; who could not weep at the horror, the horror of it all.

Within a few hours I was numb and cold and utterly uncom-
prehending. How, how could this have happened? Why, why
did it happen? How could the world have let this happen?
How could God have let this happen? How could God be
good and let the Holocaust happen? But even as my mind
silently screamed these questions, the words of a German
Jewish philosopher of the twentieth century, Edith Stein, who
had moved from Judaism to atheism to phenomenology to
Christianity to Roman Catholicism to becoming an enclosed
Carmelite nun who, ironically was sent by the Nazis to
Auschwitz where she died in the gas-chambers; the words of
Edith Stein, whom I had always admired came to mind,
words which she had written in her journal a short time
before her death: 'I spoke to our Saviour and told him that I
knew that it was his cross which was now being laid on the
Jewish people.' But having seen the evidence of Yad Vashem,
my trust in those words was shaken. Why would a loving
God, if such he was, place such a cross on his people, his chosen people? Surely no father would give his children a gift
that would maim and torture and destroy them? Yet that was
what God had done. Did it make sense to see the Holocaust
as Edith Stein did, as the gift of the cross?

I pushed open the door of another building. It was the Art
Museum. After the crushing catalogue of horrors of the last
few hours, the Art Museum proved to be the kiss of life. For
as I wandered from room to room, I began to be filled with
awe and admiration and pride at the courage and resilience
of the Jewish people. Here in these rooms were sculptures,
paintings, drawings and etchings done in the ghettos, in the
concentration camps, in the years after the Holocaust; each
one in its own way bearing witness to a will to endure in the
human spirit; to a spark of defiant courage which gave life
through art. Sculptures, paintings, drawings, etchings ... all
manifested what the Nazis could not destroy: the Jewish spirit.
Here were the voices calling from the wilderness, explaining

what it was all about; explaining that the Holocaust could kill the bodies but could not touch the souls of the Jewish people. Yad Vashem itself was a gigantic testimony to the vitality of those who perished and to those who kept their memories alive; a testimony to the vitality that is called 'soul'.

And it was here amidst these testimonies of what is noblest in human nature that I realised that 'the cross' was the Christian category which made suffering comprehensible; but only to those who believed in the divinity of Christ, as Edith Stein did, whose Christian response to the Holocaust was: 'It is His cross which is being laid on the Jewish people'. But there, on the wall of the Art Museum of Yad Vashem, was one picture which directly confronted the words of Edith Stein and challenged the Christian interpretation of Jewish history. In black and white tones the artist had painted a long, long road, along which marched hundreds of Jews, headed for Auschwitz or Dachau or Bergen-Belsen which was way in the distance. But the last Jew in the line had turned around and, hand outstretched, reached out towards a cross which was standing at the side of the road, to which was nailed Jesus of Nazareth; and he pulled at Jesus' hand, half pulling his body from the cross. The message was the image, not the word, but its essence was clear: 'Come and be really crucified with your people, Jesus – since you too are a Jew.'

Looking at that picture I felt as if I was struck by a bolt of lightening. Gazing at it for a long time, barely able to breathe, I forced my lips to move, to utter the words that welled up from the depths of my being: 'This is the truth.' For how could anyone be moved by the sufferings of Jesus when one saw what the Jewish people had suffered in the Holocaust? How long had Jesus hung on the cross? Three hours? Four hours? Five hours? But what were those few hours compared to days and weeks and months and years of agony, being hounded and slaughtered in the ghettos; being packed like cattle into trains that took them to the death-camps; being stripped, being beaten, being tortured, being experimented upon; being raped, being shot, being hung, being gassed; being melted into bars of soap? What were the sufferings of Jesus of Nazareth compared to those of his people – even if he truly was the Son of God? And if he truly was the Son of God, were his sufferings not even less than if he was simply a human being, for did he not know with absolute certainty that he would rise again in three days and sit at the right hand of the Father? But his people had no such certainty. All they had was the horror of what they had to endure; and then, unbelievably, they found the courage to express that horror and in so doing, conquered it.

The nature and heritage of Jesus of Nazareth is problematic for many Christians. It had always troubled me in a way, but I somehow accepted it because I had been born into a Christian milieu. But in Yad Vashem I felt as if a veil were rent from my eyes and that the direction of my life had to change utterly. And as I sat on the hillside near the Children's Memorial I heard over and over again in my mind the words of an old woman at home in Kerry whom I had met some weeks previously, who had said bitterly: 'If I were God, I'd be a lot kinder and more merciful than him.' I knew just how she felt, because I felt it now too, and I knew that from now on, I was going to have nothing more to do with such a heartless God. From that moment on, I repudiated him completely.

I left Yad Vashem in utter bewilderment and went back to Dublin. No amount of persuasion from the trail of symbols throughout history telling me that there was such a human phenomenon as closure to the divine ground, and that I was experiencing it in yet another of its manifestations, could impinge on the white anger that gnawed at the core of my being. I carried on with my work as usual, though I was eaten up inside with a combination of hatred and anger and despair. The weeks and months that followed were a kind of hell. Then I got a telephone call from home telling me that one of my cousins, Tommy, had gone to St James Hospital because he had a form of leukaemia, and would I go and visit him. He was one of my younger cousins, a good ten years younger than me, and I hadn't met him for years. I remembered three small boys, Tommy and his two brothers, playing with my younger brothers from time to time and was worried that I wouldn't recognise him when I went to visit. But I did; he hadn't changed that much though he was older of course, about twenty-two at that stage. He was a very quiet lad, and quite calm about being in St James, though it was obvious that everybody in that ward was very ill. When I first went to see him, I found it difficult to believe that he was, in fact, ill. He looked well and healthy, with lovely thick dark hair, and very dark eyes which radiated calmness. We got on well, despite the generation gap. But when I visited him again, he was bald. He had started chemotherapy, and rather than wait for his hair to fall out, he had his head shaved. I admired his courage. You felt, here is someone who is facing what life is subjecting him to, and challenging it. He kept a rosary on his bedside locker, and though he never spoke about God or religion, you got a sense that he had a deep steady faith which was with him the whole time. But as time went by his condition deteriorated and he had to have a bone marrow transplant. His brother James came up from Kerry and had the marrow taken out of his back for the transplant. I was awed by the matter-of-fact way he dealt with it, even though he too was in some pain for a time afterwards. For a while everything seemed to be fine. Tommy was looking forward to going back to Kerry and looking after the cows again, and going to the local football matches. But he worsened, and worsened, and he was quite conscious of his own deterioration.

The last time I saw him in the intensive care unit of St James hospital, his body had broken down and he was unconscious. I just burst into tears when I saw how much he was suffering. I left the intensive care unit in anguish, and hurried along the corridors of St James in floods of tears, almost out of my mind. What could I do to help him, to ease his suffering? There was nothing. I stumbled along almost blinded by tears and found my way to the chapel in the hospital. I went in, right up to the front row and collapsed into it. Please, please help him, I just begged and begged God. Please, please help him. I stayed there a long time, sobbing my heart out. But when I left I was calm and at peace with myself and with God and I knew that Tommy would be taken care of, very tenderly.

A few days later, he died. It was heartbreaking for his mother and father and brothers and sister, for his girl-friend, for his friends and relations and everybody who knew him. It was just heartbreaking.

But had Tommy not lived and suffered and died as he did, I would be a different person today. Because when I saw how ill he was and how terribly he suffered, I wanted to help him and found that I was powerless to do so. So I ran to the only person I knew who had the power to help him and who would help him, because he knew what suffering and pain was all about, Jesus Christ. It didn't matter that he had died two thousand years ago. His spirit lived on. Only a god who suffered and died a horribly painful death as he did could truly understand what it was to be human and to suffer and die in that way and feel the anguish such suffering left in its wake. Only a god who suffered can truly save us. And that God is the Unknown God discerned by the prophets and the philosophers and the gurus and the yogis; the God who made himself known in the person of Jesus Christ. Only a God made human can understand all the turmoil and anguish provoked by the human condition, because he has lived and died through it. That includes the suffering of those like Tommy and his family and friends, and the people who suffered in Northern Ireland, in Bosnia, in Algeria, in Calcutta, in Africa as well as the suffering of the Jews and all those who died during the Holocaust; it includes all the known and unknown suffering in the world.

Afterwards, a long time afterwards, what I had hurled at God in Yad Vashem, 'Come and be really crucified, Jesus, for you too are a Jew' even though it was what the painting seemed to say to me, reminded me – shamefully reminded me – of the taunts hurled at Christ on the cross by the thief on his left-hand side who derided him saying:

'Are you not the Messiah? Save yourself and us!'

But even though I am full of shame when I remember my words, I can understand why I said them or why anyone would say them who was driven by terrible and despairing suffering, such as that thief was. But now, it seems to me to be a terribly cruel attitude to press on to someone who was suffering too.

For they were my words, mine and no-one else's. I discovered that the next year when I returned to Jerusalem, this time at peace with myself. I came back to do pilgrimage, to see the places where Christ had lived and died, so that I might come to a better knowledge and understanding of him. But one day, I left the group and made my own way to Yad Vashem. I don't know why I wanted to visit it again; I just knew that it was somewhere I had to go. When I got there I went first to the Art Museum. But I couldn't find my painting, the painting of the line of Jews walking towards a concentration camp, with the last Jew in the line reaching out to a cross which was standing at the side of the road and half-pulling Jesus's body from the cross; the picture which evoked from me the words, 'Come and be really crucified with your people, Jesus, for you too are a Jew.' That painting was not there. Maybe it never was there; maybe it never existed. However, what was there was something very similar: a painting in black and white of a line of Jews walking towards a death-camp, and the rear of the line was brought up by a Nazi who reached out towards a cross at the side of the road and pulled Jesus towards the line.

It was part of a series of paintings by a Hungarian Jewish

artist named Moshe Hoffman, a series called the '6,000,001'. I knew who the six million were – the Jews who had perished during the Holocaust – and I knew who the one was too, Jesus Christ. All of Moshe Hoffman's prints were variations on the theme of the cross in the concentration camps. And it was this Jewish artist, about whom I know very little, who opened my eyes to the depths of the wounds and the flaws in myself, and helped me to understand my relationship with God. During my first visit to Yad Vashem when I looked at his paintings which touched such a deep chord within me, I saw what I wanted to see: I saw a God who deserved to suffer, because I considered that he hadn't suffered enough – even though I didn't really know that I felt this, and had felt it, since Grandmother's death. Of course I knew, consciously knew, that I had been bitter and angry with God from time to time since then. But I had no idea how deep that sense of bitterness and anger and hatred went, until I visited Yad Vashem. Moshe Hoffman's painting drew me forth; it was not I who drew anything from it. It drew forth my wounded sight and my wounded heart, wounded on Christmas Day when I was sixteen years old and in so doing, enabled me to hurl the taunt that had been hidden in the depth of my being all those years, the taunt that he hadn't suffered enough – because he hadn't suffered as I had. I was the last person in the line who pulled at Jesus's hand saying: 'Come and be really crucified, Jesus – since you too are a human being.'

But now I knew otherwise, thanks to my cousin Tommy. If I hadn't seen that gentle young man suffer and die as he did, I would not have been touched to my heart to want to help him; so touched that I knew instinctively that only a God who suffered can save us from the pain of our human suffering, and I went to kneel at that God's feet, with a new heart and mind and spirit. Since that time, I know why I am a Christian and why I want to be a Christian. Knowing that, knowing what I know through the whole experience of my life: that the Unknown God became known as a human being, as an infinitely attractive character from the Galilee region named Jesus, who shared our humanity in all its beauty and awfulness, yet who did so to let us know that he understood us and was with us, would always be with us in our times of need; knowing that, because I have experienced that, is the rock and anchor of my life.

So I was saddened when on the Davis show on RTE television a few weeks ago on a discussion on God and spirituality, one of the participants, a humanist named Dr Paddy Leahy, said that having read the Bible, he was convinced that Yahweh was 'the greatest sadistic savage that ever lived.' Moreover, he thought that 'Pol Pot and Hitler were all angelic compared to Yahweh.' I was saddened because I had experienced that terrible aspect of God's nature too, that aspect which is incomprehensible to my mind and probably to Dr Leahy's. But I was fortunate to have experienced the revelation of that Unknown God in the known God-man, Jesus Christ, and that has made all the difference. Until I returned to Yad Vashem after my cousin Tommy's death, I never knew how much my life-experience had coloured my relationship with God. Not knowing what Dr Leahy's deepest experiences are, I have no idea why he cannot relate to God, but instead has chosen the stoical path of humanism by which to live. It is the experience of so many others too. But because it was mine also; because the most intense experiences of my life have been those of the absence or coldness or aloofness or downright hard-heartedness of God and because I was shattered through them, I would like to be able to show Dr Leahy and others like him the loving God whom I have come to know in the person of Jesus Christ . But I know that that cannot be done. No amount of saying: 'Look, there he is' can do that because our lives and the paths along which we walk are so uniquely different. The only thing one can hope for is that others will look in the direction we indicate and explore it for themselves.

Yad Vashem, which is the memorial to the victims of the

Holocaust in Jerusalem, means 'a monument and a name.' It
comes from the book of Isaiah (56:5) where the Lord says:

'Let not the foreigner say,
Who has attached himself to the Lord,
'The Lord will keep me apart from his people';
And let not the eunuch say,
'I am a withered tree.'
For thus said the Lord:
'As for the eunuchs who keep my sabbaths,
Who have chosen what I desire
And hold fast to my covenant –
I will give them, in my House
And within my walls,
A monument and a name
Better than sons or daughters.
I will give them an everlasting name
Which shall not perish.'

After Tommy's death when I visited Yad Vashem once again,
I found a quiet place to sit and grieve for a while. But my tears
were not tears of sadness only. They were also tears of hope;
hope that through the monument and the name which drew
me to itself, that drew visitors from all over the world, the
light of the human spirit would never be extinguished –
because it was ignited by a fire greater than anything man
could make or conceive of. And there was also hope because
now I had seen that there is another way of being a monument and a name that manifests and utters hope to the world,
and that is by the testimony of one's life. My cousin Tommy's
life was such a testimony. And in a different way, so was
Grandmother's. Nothing can wipe away the awful loneliness
of her death, or of Kitty's death either. But now I am sure that
the God who himself knew what it was to feel utterly forsaken
and alone would, above all people and gods everywhere,
have known how Grandmother felt that Christmas night and
understood how she was overcome by the darkness of

despair, as Kitty was. So would he, knowing what it was to cry out 'My God, my God, why have you forsaken me?' have abandoned her? Would he have abandoned them? No. He did not abandon me, so why would he abandon them, or Tommy or the Jews who suffered or anyone who suffers, any-where, at any time? He who loved in such an excellent way could so love because he was love; is love, and shall be love for each and everyone of us, forever. That is why I am a Christian, why I want to be a Christian, and why I try after every failed attempt, to begin again to be a Christian. I need his love. Without it, the world would be a dark and lonely place. But though admitting to myself to needing such love has brought peace to my life, it does not answer all my ques-tions. I will never understand why Grandmother killed her-self on Christmas night, the night hope came into the world, or why he let her do it, anymore than I will ever understand why he let the Holocaust happen even though it happened to his own blood-family, the Jews. Nor will I ever understand why he let Tommy die, young, handsome, gentle Tommy, and let so many other people, much older people, people who had a good innings, live to an even riper old age. There is so much that I don't understand; the same kind of things that I didn't understand when I was sixteen and which drove me to despair as a result. Now those same things remain as mysteri-ous as ever; but now I know that there is so much that I will never understand.

These reflections were initiated by a kind of pebble in a pond, by an event that created ripples so wide that they eventually touched me. That event was President Mary Robinson's wearing a green dress with a sprig of mimosa in her brooch when she had a private audience with Pope John Paul II in the Vatican earlier this year. In the publicity and correspon-dence following that meeting, to which I contributed, Virginia Kennerley wrote a letter in *The Irish Times* with three questions for me, which fell around me like three hand-grenades going off. They touched on issues that I had never even thought of, let alone thought to explore. Exploring them has been a journey into the depths, of which Heraclitus long ago said was so deep that you could not travel the length of it so deep was its *logos*. I don't understand why I have been given my life, but I have come to an acceptance that it has been given to me so that I can experience love; not only the love of those I love, but the love of the God of love, so that I too, may share that love with others in whatever way I can, wherever I am. Love alone abides and out of the darkness of the past, love gleams like a star in the night sky, directing the course of the present and the future by its light.